A Business Owner's Practical Guide to Cybercrime and Business Continuity

A simplified overview of how to avoid becoming a victim and what you can do proactively to avoid losing your data, time, money and business

ISBN-13: 978-1517513030
ISBN-10: 1517513030

Printed in the USA.

Business Owner
Computer Guru
Published Author
Public Speaker

Fred Holzsager

Author of
All Systems GO: *Secrets You Need to Know About Hiring a*
Top-Notch Computer Consultant for Hassle-Free Computing
and
A Business Owner's Practical Guide to
Cybercrime and Business Continuity

Your Success is Our Success

Fred Holzsager
Holzsager Technology Services, LLC
13-15 Broadway
Fair Lawn, NJ 07410
201-797-5050
fred@tech4now.com

www.tech4now.com/cybercrime

"A must read for anyone working at a small business. Cybersecurity and cybercrime are big problems facing every business today, yet they are often ignored. Fred does a great job explaining what the issues are and how to address them."

—Art Gross, CEO,
HIPAA Secure Now!

"With many years of experience in the field of information technology, Fred has provided his readers with a very informative, practical guide to running a business in a world faced with countless technological challenges. This book offers many examples of the threats faced by small business owners every day along with clear and concise strategies for keeping critical data secure. Written for the non-techy business professional, this book requires a minimal investment in time but provides an astonishing amount of insight that would be appreciated by even the most seasoned IT professional."

—Gary Habel, President,
DIS Technologies

"Fred has written an insightful and informative technical account of two extremely important and interrelated business topics, Cybercrime and Business Continuity. He has done an exceptional job offering a practical road map for understanding and managing these critical business issues. I highly recommend that anyone involved with or responsible for managing a business take the time to read Fred's book to appreciate and prepare for the challenges that lie ahead."

—Ed Timmes, President,
Precision Sales & Business Automation, Inc.

"Fred's book is fast paced and to the point. He gets to the heart of the matter using great examples. He defines the terms so there is no confusion. This is a great framework for anyone who wants

to build a plan to protect their business. Fred leaves no stone unturned making this a complete "how to" guide. Fred's years of experience in the IT field shine through. He leaves nothing to chance. Reading this book and following its instructions will make any business more secure in these troubling times. This is a Game Plan for your business.

As an IT professional, speaker, and author, Fred is uniquely qualified to help small businesses protect themselves and prosper. This is a must read if you have security concerns about your business and who doesn't?"

**—Robert H. Springer, Solutions Architect,
BusinessTechTeam**

"In this book, Mr. Holzsager points out some ways that your computer and its data may be compromised. Proper controls can safeguard your valuable resource and inherent data from wrongful manipulation or deletion. This book can help the novice and/or computer professional increase their awareness of computer scams, breaches and/or computer exposures. It is up to you to maintain a defensive posture against computer breaches. I highly recommend this text as a fast reading guide for maintaining safe computing."

**—Bruce Rein,
Cyber Security and IT Compliance Consultant,
Deutsche Bank**

"As an IT professional with over 40 years in the industry, I found this to be one of the most readable books pertaining to issues of prevention, detection and recovery from all forms of disaster, both intentional and inadvertent. It appreciates the fact that the audience probably has limited technical expertise, but solid experience in running the business. Rather than focusing on technical jargon, it considers that business continuity encompasses protection of information, communication planning, deployment of human resources, damage assessment, supply

*chain continuity, insurance protection and safety. It deals intelligently with **all** of the areas that require attention, with the goal of planning and being able to execute all of the tasks needed to get a business up and running after any time of malicious incursion, unintentional breach or act of nature that may impact normal operations of the business. This is not a bits and bytes book, but rather an excellent survival guide written with a sometimes whimsical sense of humor."*
                    —Alan Eliscu, Independent IT Consultant Specializing in Data Architecture and Information Management

*"With the fast pace of technology and public & private sector data breaches commanding more headlines on a national level, cyber security has developed into a competitive priority. The increasing need for deliberate disaster preparedness is a new business 'normal.' One of the most prolific threats for businesses is to ignore vulnerabilities, without developing contingency plans for immediate deployment. "**Cybercrime and Business Continuity**" by Fred Holzsager articulates where many key areas may experience a loss: data security, customer and client data, and smooth business operations. Such oversights may damage the business' legitimacy, client and customer loyalty, and may be "unforgivable" in a competitive business environment. This book is an easy read and defines areas in cyber security relevant to any small business with a rich and simplified approach."*
                    —Vincent J. Vicari, Regional Director, NJSBDC at Bergen County

Table of Contents

Acknowledgements

This book is dedicated to my dear, adoring family, wonderful clients and those who toil day in and day out to support their families by running small businesses. I also want to thank those who helped me to compile this work: Debra Broseker and the members of my accountability groups. Reviewing this book for errata and syntax errors was also a chore, for this, I want to recognize the time spent and results shared by Gary Holzsager, Celeste Allen, Bruce Rein, Robert Springer (BusinessTechTeam), Alan Eliscu and Ed Timmes (Precision SBA), all of whom shared their findings and corrections in a kind, spirited manner. I also wish to acknowledge the contributions to this book from Vincent J. Vicari (Regional Director of *NJ Small Business Development Center* (Bergen County)), Steven Gutkin (Associate Director of *NJ Office of Homeland Security & Preparedness*), Steven S. Rubin, Esq. (Moritt Hock & Hamroff), Shiraz Saeed (Cyber Product Specialist at AIG), Pat Felicetta (HIPAASecureNow and PII Protect), Rena Bernstein (Elektrik Ink) for the cover art and the folks at Datto Backup who so graciously endowed the printing of this first edition.

Last, but not least, I wish to acknowledge the lessons my parents taught me about being safe and contributing to the community to make it a better place for everyone.

Foreword

When Fred reached out to me to tell me he was writing a book on Business Continuity and all the risks and cybercrime that go along with that, I was excited for a couple of different reasons. First, Fred and his team are genuine experts in this field. Secondly, this area is talked about a lot, but very little action or planning is put into place or documented.

Cybercrime, cloud security, data risk and business continuity have become some of the most critical parts of any business today, ranging from small to medium to large businesses. We've seen small shops deal with theft; we've seen large shops deal with ransomware and everything in between.

Datto is one of the world leaders in data continuity and as a result, we're continuously reviewing the reasons why our customers need to recover data in these disaster scenarios. What we've found is that 97% of all data restores are done as a result of humans. That includes employee error within the business itself, physical crimes such as theft and of course cybercrimes.

In September 2013, I saw my first glimpse of CryptoLocker. I contacted our Support Team and asked how many restores due to this new type of attack we have done, and the answer was zero. About two weeks later, I got a call from the same team saying we had just completed our thousandth restore due to CryptoLocker. This is how quickly we've seen cybercrime evolve and how important the need for data protection truly is.

I personally have seen significant evolution in the way in which your networks are being managed and therefore, being threatened. As technology continues to evolve, so do those trying to attack it for malicious reasons.

As a result, the most successful businesses at keeping these attacks to a minimum and maintaining uptime need to stay on top of the ever changing and evolving technologies. Fred and his team are leaders in doing so.

With the rapid adoption of cloud technology and the lack of awareness, understanding and vendor diligence when positioning the cloud, not only are the threats greater, there are significantly more opportunities and avenues for people to attack.

I thoroughly enjoyed this book you're about to read and look forward to seeing more from Fred as our industry and the technology in it continues to evolve.

Rob T. Rae
Vice President of Business Development
Datto
www.datto.com

"If I am not for myself,

who will be for me?

But, if I am only for myself,

what am I?

(And) if not now, when?"

— Hillel The Elder

"If you learn a lesson from this book, I hope it will be to become aware of what you and your business are going through at any moment, whether you are under attack, experiencing a disaster, thriving or simply making your organization resilient to what fate has in store for you. May you gain the needed know-how from this book to endure."

Fred W. Holzsager
Holzsager Technology Services

Characteristic Definition:

Cybercrime: Also known as *computer crime* or *net crime*, is loosely defined as any criminal activity that involves a computer and a network, whether in the commissioning of the crime or as the target.

Cybercrime Overview

Building a business is a long and exhaustive process. Every day, businesses fall victim to cyber thieves through scams such as *phishing*, *Trojans*, *keyboard loggers* and *CryptoLocker* implementations to mention a few. We have been in business for over thirteen years and during that time, we have seen a growth in incidences as well as a rise in the level of sophistication implemented by cyber thieves.

We have witnessed how well-meaning end users have been cajoled into releasing their personal and sensitive information to those whose intention is less than wholesome. These end users are like you and me. They are not gullible or simpleminded; however, they are readily deceived by carefully scripted *social engineering*.

You may say to yourself, "I'm smarter than those people and I'm not going to fall for any trick from a two-bit thief in a third world country," but, it is not that way. The scams are often more deceptive than you may have imagined. Some are not even going to involve you in an interactive way, they will just launch a program (*worm*) on your machine and you will be the next victim. Others will use your human nature against you—for example, your curiosity may become your downfall.

At the onset of a spotted attack, companies used to assume that the victim [user of the system] was visiting a porn site; however, if a porn site wants a continuous flow of visitors, infecting their [visitors'] machines repeatedly would not be a great choice of marketing/PR. It is reasonable to presume these attacks were not necessarily sourced by a pornographic patron.

Using the Front Door to enter the premises

One of the most common techniques to infiltrate a network may be using a "*dropped USB drive or DVD.*" The way this method works is straight forward and plays on your nature to either return the key/disk to someone who may have lost it or to see what may be confidential or private on a lost piece of hardware. Imagine you are walking down a hall or through a parking lot, look down and find a USB key. What goes through your mind when you see it? Are you going to plug it into a computer in your home? In your office? Leave it behind and post a FOUND notice for someone to claim it (allowing that party to retain their full privacy by NOT plugging it in?). In most cases, the latter is less than likely.

Did you know that operating systems like Windows XP and newer introduced a feature to allow you to connect a USB and NOT have it immediately launch upon being attached? Is it enabled on your network? Was it enabled when you looked at the contents of that USB key you found? Did you fight the temptation to peek or did you succumb to curiosity?

The attack described above is similar to the Trojan Horse story. The Greeks build an oversized wooden horse and deliver it to Troy. Many of the Trojans question why the statue of the horse is presented, yet it finds its way into the city. As the story goes, it is a ploy in which elite Greek soldiers are hiding to attack Troy from within. In the case of the USB drive, you find a "gift" (Trojan Horse), attach it to your computer (bring the gift into the secure confines of your network), then leave its payload in your premises (attack executed internally by violating code (soldiers) when least expected). You are now, unknowingly, sharing your private data with anonymous entities that will use your information to their exclusive benefit.

What are they looking for?

In many situations, the trespassers are looking for either competitive data or personal holdings information. This attack may allow a hostile country to bring down a state-funded development of centrifuges (*StuxNet* virus); allow an identity thief to acquire funds from your bank or investment accounts by ordering new credit cards, emulating your login to an account to effect a withdrawal or destroying your reputation by mimicking you in a forum and posting unkind or inappropriate comments to the forum members (including Facebook etc.).

On other occasions, it may simply be a program that tracks your keystrokes and reports them back to the "mother ship" to use in impersonating you in any situation that does not require a face-to-face interaction. This last example is that of a keyboard logger.

The recent trend in online piracy comes from the CryptoWall or CryptoLocker viruses. These viruses are reputed to be the final phase of a process to squeeze out the most from a victim. In this situation, the victim has, most likely, been a victim of the Trojan or keyboard logger and has provided information that was already tapped. Now, as the culminating action, a trigger is enabled to have the victim's data encrypted and held for ransom.

How is this done?

Remember, this machine had already been hijacked and exploited because it was infiltrated. With gainful access to the machine, the cyber thieves enable/launch codes which take all files that would be considered data (e.g., documents, financials, spreadsheets, PDFs, drawings and photographs) and encrypt them with a special key. This key, by the way, can be readily acquired by the victim for a price. Once it is paid, the victim is then given instructions on how to decrypt the files to regain access.

NOTE: *The scariest aspect of this process is that by the time the* CryptoLocker *phase is invoked, the machine has typically been reviewed by a minimum of three to four other viruses which gleaned and applied the information found for other purposes.*

Three questions remain:

1. How do I recover ALL of my encrypted files? (often, not all files will decrypt successfully).

2. Now that I have decrypted the files, what assures me that the same party will not do this to me again based on them still having their code resident on my machine?

3. Am I encouraging kidnapping of data if I pay this, even once?

The entities running this scheme recognize the fact that if they only take the ransom and do NOT allow the victims to recover data, they will be unable to collect monies in the future. Their challenge was to determine HOW they would collect money from the victims that would be difficult, if not impossible, to trace.

How do the CryptoLocker and CryptoWall coders collect their ransoms without being traced?

If you are a victim of the CryptoWall or CryptoLocker virus, you may have an option with which to pay. Because these transactions cannot be effected in person, cash is not an option. So, what is a resourceful thief to do?

• **PayPal** – this is not the option of choice for the extortionist, but still leaves the thief with a chance to collect anonymously. If you are hit by the "Cryptos," paying with PayPal will often come at a premium because it is potentially reversible.

• **BitCoin (BTC)** – the "currency" of choice was developed by Satoshi Nakamoto in 2008. A description of Bitcoin can be found at *https://en.wikipedia.org/wiki/Bitcoin* online. We are also including some of that information in the back of this guide in the Glossary.

The beauty of working with these thieves that imprison your data with encryption is that, once they have received your ransom payment and have effected the "release" (decryption) of your data, they send you a cordial thank you note and wish you to "have a nice day." As unscrupulous as they may be, it appears their moms taught them to always be polite. *Ouch!*

In case you were wondering how you got the CryptoWall or CryptoLocker in the first place, the likelihood has shown that it usually arrives as an email attachment, often in a .ZIP format (that's the DISPLAYED extension) and the files usually have a name that pertains to a transaction (*e.g.,* "invoice.zip" or "receipt.zip"). Thus, the next time you receive an email that has no apparent addressee (*e.g.*, "Dear Customer" or "For You"), let your spider sense start tingling and alerting you to a red flag item that you should approach with caution. In fact, a few years ago, there were some viruses that were so tenacious, even clicking on the file to view its properties, not executing it, would cause it to launch. Give it time, one can only expect improvements in the implementation of these attacks.

How do the cyberthieves create so many attacks?

If you launch a browser and go to Google.com, you will see that entering the search term, "how to create a virus file" or "Exploit Kit" and you will find instructions, sample code, YouTube videos, kits and clubs to join. Many of the sites resemble:

- *HackersOnlineClub.com*
- *ComputerVirus.uw.hu*
- *CoolHackingTrick.com*
- *EngineersGarage.com*
- *Virus.Wikidot.com/virus-generator*
- *HackWithMak.com*
- *Spth.virii.lu*
- *ComputerHope.com*
- *VXHeaven.org*
- *GoHacking.com*

The list goes on and on. You can find more, the list is only limited by your imagination at devising names to search for.

> **NOTE**: Even though you may have located sites that appear to be what you seek, there is no telling whether these sites will either report your IP back to a governing body or will actually launch an "injection" of code onto your machine. We strongly advise AGAINST performing this search and visiting the discovered sites. *You may get more than you bargained for.*

"Well, that's another fine mess you've gotten me into"

—Laurel and Hardy

Are they *clairevoyant* or something?

The other day, I was enjoying a meal with my family when the phone rang. My wife happened to answer the call. There was a woman on the line with an accent telling her the computer was infected and could possibly be destroyed by a virus. She urged my wife to open a browser to allow her to connect and fix the problem. She started to tell her a web address to go to before my wife mentioned that her computer was off and not in use.

"How can you tell what my computer is doing if it is turned off and not online?" my wife asked.

"We received a message from your antivirus indicating you had a virus. You must allow me to connect to your computer, otherwise, you may lose all of your data."

"Could you tell me which antivirus I am using, so I know you are who you say you are?" my wife added.

"It doesn't matter which one you are using, all of them tell us when a virus attacks your machine. You must connect to the website I'll give you in order for me to connect to your machine. Your time is running out!" the caller responded.

Click. [My wife hung up the phone on her.]

Under closer review (no microscope required)

As incredibly bold as it may sound, the above exchange actually occurred. You might feel tempted to work with such a proactive technician, but beware of such a call, it is not as friendly as you may believe.

This scam is perpetrated on a frequent basis. We typically receive 1-2 calls for this matter on a monthly basis and the common thread to the victim list is that these are people who are insecure to an extent with computers and the way they work.

As you may have guessed, if my wife's machine was turned off, it was not online beaconing a distress call through the antivirus agent. The computer is as likely to send a signal to this woman as you would be to telephone her while you are asleep or under anesthesia. Plain and simple—it's not happening. Second, the fact that she called our home to notify us, albeit remotely feasible, was not likely. Although the marketing departments of the security software companies would love to have our phone number for solicitation purposes (if provided, it may be construed as an "opt-in."), we do not provide the home phone number to them, so the odds of her having our number to call under such circumstances are less likely than being attacked by a shark while reclining in a chair in your living room. Third, if she were calling on behalf of a company in such a proactive manner, wouldn't this be the prime opportunity to make them shine by stating their name and citing this as a salient benefit of being their customer? – Strike three!

Constantly vigilant

In today's electronic world, you must learn to see and hear the tell tale signs of a scam. Thieves have become far more sophisticated in their techniques by introducing social engineering and the application of behavior modification to their arsenals. Now, when you are online, quietly working on your computer, you must be aware of even the most subtle indication that something is just "not right" with your e-mail message or that website you recently visited. Not only is your common sense the first line of defense, so is an education and level of awareness.

For example, you work with a small group of friends in an organization. The popular practice is to share your collaborative documents and notes through Dropbox. You send messages frequently advising each other to visit the Dropbox to review an update or to add your share of insights to the latest document. It works great and you are making tremendous strides in productivity. Then, you receive an e-mail from a "colleague" indicating that they have a new document. There is no descriptive text in the message, but there is a hyperlink to "Dropbox link."

In general, whenever you have communicated within the group, you have placed a description in the subject line of the email. You have also named the documents and included their names in the links. Something is off with this message, but you just can't place it. You have the link on your screen in Outlook and the mouse cursor happens to hoover over the link, then the actual address is displayed:

https://drop.box/questionable-venue.ro
/k/sr45tghkq/Cybersaftey.pdf

(Besides the fact that dropbox is now separated by a period; note that the word "Cybersafety" is misspelled. Furthermore, the country code for this link is "RO" (Romania). All warning signs.)

If you were to actually send an invitation to a colleague to review or access your Dropbox share, it would look more like this...

https://www.dropbox.com/s/ksbwua13jxormnq /Cybersafety.jpg?dl=0

It is up to your vigilance to recognize the "anomalies" that appear to tip you off to the fact that they are not genuine.

So many people have been attacked over time that the government has enacted legislation which is designed to have companies control and maintain privacy for individuals. The nature of most virus attacks is to steal or compromise data on computers. That data is then sold on the black market to those who convert the information into new credit cards and identity mechanisms such as driver licenses or passports. This practice, over time, has become a major concern that the state and federal governments viewed as a significant concern, so laws were enacted to punish those who transport or store that information in an insecure manner.

Companies have developed techniques and storage devices designed to thwart the thieves by either encrypting the data or storing it in protected locations that are "relatively impenetrable" as verified by penetration testers (often done by ethical hackers).

One of the other ways to protect yourself from fines and other penalties for storing personally identifiable information (PII) is by scanning your computer to confirm or identify its presence on your computer. There are programs available to help you scan your machine for the presence of PII and assess the potential liability you carry by it being resident on your machines. This also applies to smartphones, tablets, laptops and other portable devices.

"Where an educated consumer is our best customer."
   —Sy Merns (Syms)

FYI: We are a service partner for the product ***PII Protect*** that not only enables you to discover threats, but trains you in how to recognize the signs. If you are interested in learning more about this, please see our special offer at the back of the book to learn how you may benefit from this service.

If you suspect your computer may have social security, driver license or credit card numbers and would like to remove or encrypt them, please feel free to contact us to participate in this program. We can help you avoid the possible penalties and give you an accurate assessment of the potential fine values associated with each of the items stored improperly on your systems. Not only will you have your systems assessed, but the program also includes security training for all of your staff as well as up to $100,000 of insurance protection to help you should you need it due to a breach. For more details on this product, visit ***http://www.tech4now.com/pii-protect***.

Striking Example

Have you ever had your personal information breached? Visit the site at the <u>New York Times</u> to view your victim potential.

http://www.nytimes.com/interactive/2015/07/29/technol ogy/personaltech/what-parts-of-your-information- have-been-exposed-to-hackers-quiz.html?smid=tw- share&_r=4

As you review your results from the aforementioned assessment, you will notice that they make one salient point...

Q: How can you protect yourself in the future?

A: It's pretty simple: You can't. But you can take a few steps to make things harder for criminals. (Read the notes on the quiz for further insights.)

Besides giving you useful suggestions, the page also includes links to articles about all of the referenced breaches and lessons learned from them. Be sure to give them a read, too!

A True Story

*The names have been changed to protect
the innocent and companies involved*

Ron was a smart, business savvy individual. He was young by comparison to most at his level in business. He and his company took standard precautions to be safe online. They used an *Internet Security* version of their security software, they use a *firewall* and they have a standard *Acceptable Use Policy* (AUP) that all employees understand and sign. Each staff member has been through training on how to be safe online. There was one glaring exception at this office, however, NO BACKUP WAS IN PLACE TO PROTECT THE COMPANY DATA.

Ron was working at his computer when he noted it was not acting normally—the system seemed slower than usual, he was having trouble opening some files and he now had a new desktop image that he had never seen before (see image on next page). The *ransomware* program, **CryptoWall 3.0**, had inhabited his machine and encrypted all of his data files. Ron called us and asked if we could undo the damage. Basically, the following happened:

An e-mail arrived for Ron in his mailbox.

The message contained an attachment named ***invoice.pdf***. These files are often given names such as "complaint," "purchase order," "office memo," or "bill" (common business communications).

The attachment was actually an executable program disguised as a PDF file. When Ron clicked on the attachment to view it in his Acrobat Reader, the program installed itself on his machine in his `%AppData%` or `%Temp%` folders.

The installer then started to scan the computer's drives for data files to encrypt. When the infection scans the computer, it scans all drive letters on the computer including removable drives, network shares, even *DropBox* mappings.

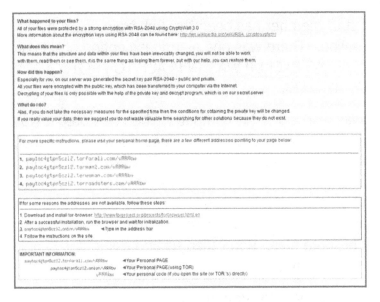

By the time we were called, it was clear that he was fully infected because the system was displaying a DOS Command window with the following line...

```
"C:\Windows\SYsWOW64\cmd.exe" /C
"C:\Windows\System32\vssadmin.exe" Delete
Shadows /All /Quiet
```

One of the techniques used by the CryptoWall is that it clears out the Shadow Copies on the computer since they can potentially restore the computer's file back to normal. By running this command, the virus eradicates all files that would normally be available without having created a true backup.

Ron looked at me and asked about his options:

- There was no image backup of his computer that could be used to restore the full computer.

- There were no file or folder backups that could be used to restore the individually affected data to their original pristine condition.

- The last copies made of the affected files were too old to use for restoration purposes—not a valid consideration.

- He could spend $500 (USD) in Bitcoin (BTC) to purchase the restoration decryption key code. Doing so would leave him with a possibly functional code, but no way to trace it or cancel the payment, let alone, take legal action.

- Unlike *CryptoLocker*, he could not pay via PayPal. The criminals were already aware that such an avenue might have given him the ability to "dispute" the payment.

- He could rebuild his computer with a clean install and start over. *That would teach them!!*

Ron decided he would purchase the *BitCoin* (BTC) to pay the ransom. His new challenge was finding a "reputable" source where he could buy them. The approximate value of $500, at the time, was 2.2BTC. Buying the BitCoin, typically, includes a processing fee, too. This quick click on the PDF was costing him more than he had bargained for.

Research was done online to try to locate a convenient BitCoin merchant in the area. He found ***www.circle.com***, an international financial company. They had him go to an office in person because he did not want to link a Circle account to his business or personal bank accounts.

The feedback on his experience was, "I went to this seedy location in The Bronx. I entered a "man trap" and gave them the cash. They gave me a note and indicated that the value was already credited to my account. I headed back to my office and finished the transaction. I had to hurry because if I was late, the price would go up to $1,000. I don't want to go through this experience ever again!!"

NOTE: THIS IS NOT AN ENDORSEMENT, it is merely provided for detail's sake. Any interaction with this company is taken at your own risk and without our recommendation.

Back at his office, he finished the transaction and received the decryption code to enter in the program's interface. The files began to appear and open. Unfortunately, not all of the files were destined to be recovered; however, compared to his mood prior, he expressed clear relief at having paid the ransom. At least now, he was still in business and did not lose some irreplaceable documents and photographs.

Lesson to be learned: Ron now makes and maintains a regular backup for all of his critical and irreplaceable files.

The cost of the time to back up your work will be more than regained when you find you need to recover the data gleaned over hours of focus and hard work—don't be "Penny-wise and pound-foolish"

This whole experience also provoked an unnerving thought... *What if the files, although decrypted, still possessed the ability to reinfect his current machine and others on his network?"*

"Fool me once, shame on you; fool me twice, shame on me."
— Randall Terry

Cybercrimes are not victimless by any measure. When a business works to prevent an event from ruining its reputation or emptying its bank accounts, it may be harmed just as extensively as the people that were on any lists that may have been harvested by the thieves.

As a business owner, you need protection from these attacks. Those that depend upon your data require you to have a reliable backup system in place to enable you to restore critical data to recover from destructive attacks. For the threats that grab data from your network, you need a different type of protection; for them, you need to have a team approach to keep you from as much devastation as possible.

If your systems are breached and you become aware of it in a timely manner, it is critical that your organization has reliable counsel, in addition to a reliable tech. *Why?* Should you ever have a tech perform a forensic review of your machines, all data that is reported may become "discoverable." Whereas, if you are breached and contact a lawyer and the attorney calls in the forensic expert, then the information provided may be construed as "attorney client privileged information" and may be defendable by your counsel. Furthermore, you will also need to do your best to protect your reputation, so a public relations contact may be needed... and don't forget to contact your insurer to help cover as much of the costs as possible. It has been documented that 60% of small & medium-sized businesses that are hit by a data breach of any significant proportion are likely to fail within 6 months of the attack. This may be attributable to the time commitment to resolve it, the financial, reputational, or emotional impact of the breach or the overall defeat of the company leadership's resolve.

It's challenging enough to run a small business. Statistics from Bloomberg indicate that most small businesses (80%) fail within their first 18 months. *Isn't that enough of a test?!* Now, besides dealing with initial aspects of growth, addressing a mile long punch-list, having to be the thought

leader for your organization and living in a virtual test environment, new entrepreneurs must face extortionist practices from rampant computer viruses. Wow, and you thought lion-taming was tough!

Creating a Strong Password

Most computer users recognize the fact that a password is often the only thing standing between the data in the account and a person trying to hack it. What can you do to improve your odds of keeping the data secure? After all, technology and law enforcement can only do so much—you need *password hygiene*.

Create a password that is difficult to guess. A hacker can guess a password by throwing a dictionary-worth of words at an account where the user name is known. This is referred to as a "dictionary attack."

In 2013, the 18 most popular passwords were:

1.	123456	7.	111111	13.	1234567890
2.	password	8.	1234567	14.	letmein
3.	12345678	9.	iloveyou	15.	photoshop
4.	qwerty	10.	adobe123	16.	1234
5.	abc123	11.	123123	17.	Monkey
6.	123456789	12.	Admin	18.	Shadow

Now, can you understand why breaches occur?!

1. If you used a password that has all lower case letters and is a word, you have a weak password. However, if you take a sentence that you can remember, extract only the first letters of each word and insert symbols and non-roman characters, you stand a better change of securing the account.

When You Bake A Pie, Try To Use Only Granny Smith Apples. Converts to "**WYB@PT#2u0G5a!**" — Here we have changed one "A" to "@", changed "to" into

#2 to note a number, kept all vowels used in lowercase letters and appended an exclamation point to enhance the 'crack' difficulty level. For any webmail or sensitive accounts, do your best to implement the most challenging passwords in your list.

2. Use two-factor authentication whenever possible. "2FA" is the method by which you have a credential/password AND a second form of identification. It may be selecting a picture, naming your first grade teacher or entering a random code generated by an authenticator. Google's Gmail and many other applications are able to incorporate either an authenticator or 2FA in your credentials to reduce the likelihood of your account being hacked. We

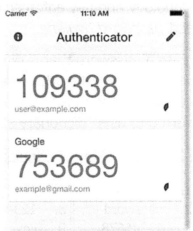

Figure 1: Google Authenticator - Note the partial circle - this is the 30 second timer to use the code. After 30 seconds, a new code appears. Code must be entered while valid to work. Get one free from Google at https://support.google.com/ accounts/answer /1066447?hl=en

know that banks now will phone your listed number with a code to enable you to provide additional proof that you are the actual person entitled to access the account.

3. Don't reuse your passwords on other accounts. Each time you repeat the use of a password, it loses its effectiveness.

4. Change your password on a regular basis. Try to do it monthly, bimonthly or quarterly at most. If you change it often, it is harder for a hacker to get at your account.

5. Consider using an online password keeper. Be advised that even though they create secure passwords for you

and are powerful tools for you to keep your data safe, the companies that provide these services have become prime targets for hackers and some have been breached (though they claim the password lists were not stolen). Some well-known password keeper programs include: Keeper® Password Manager, Password Manager Pro, Passpack, LastPass with YubiKey, Password Genie, SplashID, Roboform, DashLane, mSecure by mSeven Software, KeePass, Trend Micro DirectPass, Norton Identity Safe and MyLOK+.

Please note that we have not used any of the aforementioned Password Maintenance tools, so we cannot recommend any of them; however, they are popular and have their followings, but should not be understood to be an exhaustive list. For a relatively objective review of these utilities, we suggest you visit sites such as PCMAG.com or CNET or InformationWeek for more insight and assistance in your selection. Some of these utilities are designed for smartphones, some for PCs and some for Apple devices. Please consider your applications prior to making your purchase. For your info, some of these utilities are available for FREE.

6. As tempting as it may be, please, please, please do not write down your username and password and keep the combo affixed with a Post-It® Note to the monitor or underneath your keyboard. Believe it or not, these are the first places that hackers would check if allowed access to the premises.

Risk Assessment from an Insurer's Point of View

If you are curious as to how you may be assessed (*risk-wise*) by your insurer for any **CYBER LIABILITY**™ exposure, please review the items below.

Measure 1:

Do you handle confidential information?

- **Own Company** (including employees) – restricted data related to your business (*e.g.*, trade secrets, processes, documentation, passwords, personnel data)

- **Clients** (Confidential – personal or commercial) – agreements, pricing, financials, tax returns, photos, medical or credit cards etc.

Measure 2:

Where do you store the information?

- *Computer Network* – Do you operate it yourself onsite using your computers and servers or do you outsource to a vendor for them to store it in "The Cloud"?

- *Paper Records* – Your office has not converted all of its records from paper to electronic records. You decide, after converting it, to toss the files in the trash rather than shred them—*not a good idea!*

Measure 3:

Do you have a website?

- *What is the content on the site?* – Do you display images of patients/clients/personnel without their permission? Do you write articles that may be viewed as incriminating?

- *Can employees or third parties upload content* (*e.g.*, blog, post comments or pictures)? If you are not moderating the posts PRIOR to their appearance on your site, you may be open for libel.

Think of your cumulative score, if you answered "YES" to all three measures, your score indicates a greater risk, therefore, a higher premium to provide coverage. The key to assessment is that you are truthful; otherwise, it may come back to bite you.

The next phase is to review the factors that may affect you from an INTERNAL and an EXTERNAL standpoint.

Internally, you may work with employees and vendors. Your concerns may range from: are your internal contacts capable of MALICIOUS intent by stealing information for personal gain, sabotage due to a harbored resentment or actual financial theft through conspiracy, embezzlement or misuse of access (e.g., card skimming or inappropriate use of company credit card). These offenses may also carry possible legal action.

We also must consider those that cause an event on a casual basis through NEGLIGENCE. This often includes the misplacement or irresponsible loss of equipment bearing confidential data. If your organization did not prepare for such an incident by enabling a remote wipe or tracking, the loss of a tablet, smartphone or laptop may be your company's downfall. Again, regardless of the cause, you may be subject to legal action.

Finally, we consider the vendors working on our office equipment. When you start your relationship with them, many have you sign an agreement that stipulate all terms and conditions of engagement. If they do something "wrong," regardless of intent, you may have indemnified them, so they may have a *"get out of jail free"* card and you are *left on the hook.*

Keep in mind, with cybercrimes, you are also confronting EXTERNAL factors on a continuous basis. You may fall victim to hackers that have targeted your company due to an ethical opposition to your line of business, this is referred to as "Hacktivism." On the other hand, you may be

a victim of an outright crime committed by some type of organized crime syndicate that targets you and your staff through Spear phishing or a Distributed Denial of Service (DDoS) attack. Then, again, you might simply be hit with a virus, Trojan or keyboard logger that works in the background harvesting your internal information. They then use it until its value has diminished and then send you a time bomb that encrypts all of your data, since it is no longer of value to them (*e.g.*, "CryptoWall").

These are some of the considerations pondered by the actuaries that rate your business for the insurance industry.

Now that you are more enlightened, what are you going to do **PROACTIVELY** to prevent your business from becoming the next victim?

For your enlightenment, here are *Krebs's 3 Basic Rules for Online Safety*. This is directly from his website's blog article at krebsonsecurity.com from May 2011 (*http://krebsonsecurity.com/2011/05 /krebss-3-basic-rules-for-online-safety*).

Without listing the full article, Brian Krebs suggested the following and it makes tremendous sense to adhere to his advice...

- **Krebs's Rule #1 for Staying Safe Online:**
  "If you didn't go looking for it, don't install it!"
  You might be working on your computer when a pop-up appears with the message indicating your machine is infected by innumerous viruses and other nasties. You then get prompted to download the "suggested fix" to eliminate the scourge. Should you do it?

- **Krebs's Rule #2 for Staying Safe Online:**
  "If you installed it, update it."
  Many programs that we use on a regular basis become vulnerable to attack overtime as programmers reverse engineer the compiled codes and identify weaknesses which could lead to external systems taking control of your system or other attacks. Programs like Java, Adobe FlashPlayer, Adobe PDF Reader and QuickTime should be updated on a regular basis inasmuch as these are among the most popular software and utilities that are frequently compromised. Do you run updates on non-Microsoft applications or Microsoft Updates on your systems?

- **Krebs's Rule #3 for Staying Safe Online:**
  "If you no longer need it, remove it."
  Some companies make it a policy to remove unused software applications or those that are likely to be compromised. For example, do you remove older versions of Acrobat Reader or Java?

Mr. Krebs offers a wealth of useful articles and suggestions to help you maintain your network in a stable and safe condition. We highly recommend reading his site and visiting others that offer similar insights to running a safer network.

> *See our* **Recommended Websites** *at the end of this book.*

Other recommendations that we can offer include...

- **Enforce Strong Passwords among your employees.**
A password is most effective when it has special characters and has a length of 8 or more characters.

- **Be particular about the information you share with your vendors and business partners.**
It is your responsibility to keep track of what information is released and what is kept confidential.

- **Establish an Acceptable Use Policy (AUP) that forbids your employees from storing data on their desktops (and BYOD devices).**
By managing where your data resides, you are able to protect it better through controls and backups. Any time someone walks out of your office with a computer holding user data, you are risking the loss or compromise of that data. [*AUP Template provided on page 116 of this book.*]

- **Enroll in online alert offerings from reliable sources.**
Visit *www.us-cert.gov* for notifications on security threats.

- **Train your employees to recognize threats or scams and download only trusted applications from reputable sources.**
For more info, visit:
www.tech4now.com/pii-protect

Quick QUIZ: Below is a recent scam mail we received in our office. How many *red flags* can you identify in this message? (Answer is on Page 130)

Subject: Urgent Trip

Apologize for disturbing your moments, i came down here to Istanbul (TURKEY) for a mission program last night unfortunately on my way going back to the hotel room i got mugged all phones, cash, passport and and valuable items are in the bag they went it. The Embassy has really been helping issues for giving me a temporary passport.

Before I can head out for my flight I have to settle the hotel the bill am owing right now, i contact my bank and they get back to me with a sad reply! it will take up to 3-5 working days to access funds in my account. My flight will soon take off. I need your help/financial loan of € 2,550 Euro to sort out our hotel bill, will pay back once back home safe.

Will be very grateful, any help is appreciated

Kind Regards

Michael

Would you respond to this URGENT message or ignore it?

For your information, this was from a breached @AOL.COM email account of a business acquaintance.

Disaster Recovery

(A Business Continuity Subset)

<u>Murphy's Law</u>:
What CAN go wrong WILL go wrong at the WORST possible moment.

Now that the damage is done, what are we planning to do to maintain our business, clients, employees, building and other things that matter most to be around "tomorrow."

People often confuse *Business Continuity* (BC) with *Disaster Recovery* (DR). The statistics on Small and Medium-sized businesses (SMBs) are rather alarming – according to the Federal Emergency Management Agency (FEMA), 40% of businesses do not reopen after a disaster and another 25% fail within one year (Source: *http://www.chamber101.com/2programs_ committee/natural_disasters/disasterpreparedness /Forty.htm*, *"Business Planning for Disaster Survival"* by Corina Mullen).

Disaster Recovery is about getting your business back on its feet as quickly as possible, even if it is with a skeleton crew performing a limited number of tasks. After a significant event has affected the operation, this is done to provide a continuance of the business for the clients and to enable them to conduct business with the company in the shortest time possible.

Example of DR for a Technological Incident

There are two primary measurements that are established when creating a "DR Plan" to determine how you will run your backups – **Recovery Point Objective** (RPO) and **Recovery Time Objective** (RTO). In the diagram shown below, you see an event represented by the lightning bolt. The event may be a virus attack, a power outage, a drive failure or any number of events that simply are not planned which create the inability of your office to access critical data.

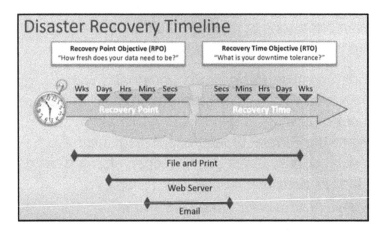

The examples have been designed to keep the terms as clear as possible. Note that the timelines compare the needs of your *Email, Web Server* and *File and Print* services.

- **Email** is typically a critical and immediate need of the business. A viable business needs to communicate within its ranks, with its client-base and with its vendors. This timeline must be restored as quickly as possible; however, the need to restore the historical email archives is not as important. The staff only has the immediate need to access recent messages and send out its responses at the earliest possible opportunity.

- **Web Server** provides the business with another channel for communicating with its clients and prospects. The [file] server is not the same as the web server (for the website). In many instances today, the Web Server is not necessarily hosted on the same location as the file server, so recovery may or may not be as adversely affected. A file server will host your data on the Local network, not on the Web.

  If a business uses its Web Server to provide access to its Remote Desktops or Terminal Server, then its level of priority rises dramatically inasmuch as it now represents almost all productivity from the company's personnel with regard to technology.

- **File and Print** refers to the business' file server and print facilities. Unless you are a commercial printer, this may not be as urgent. Consider the files you use on a daily basis, many of them, if urgent, may have been replicated in emails when sent to clients and colleagues. Thus, if the email is restored first, you may already have a restore source for your critical files. The balance of your work files, those not replicated in emails, will also need to be restored.

How can you reduce the impact of an "event"?

Planning is always a critical component of a Disaster Recovery Plan. Leaving your fate to chance in business is considered irresponsible and foolish, so here are some suggestions on giving your business greater resiliency in the event you must act on your DR Plan.

- *Install a Commercial Grade Firewall/Router –* appliances give you more control over what actual reaches your network BEFORE it arrives at your computers, so it is an effective PROACTIVE measure to keep your systems clean. Furthermore, they offer other services such as *Content Filtering* to help you maintain a non-hostile work environment for your staff and Intrusion Protection Services (IPS) with *Gateway Antivirus* and Malware Detection to deliver added protection.

- *Use an Antivirus Program to stop viruses –* many situations may require the use of an antivirus with a software firewall for added protection. Discuss this matter with your IT professional to determine what fits your situation best.

- *Use an Uninterruptible Power Supply* (UPS) for your devices – consult your IT professional if you have questions about sizing the UPS or where to install it.

- *Maintain Updates for all applications on ALL COMPUTERS* (including the Operating System!). This is the simplest, yet most widely overlooked option. Should you find this imposes a hardship, consider hiring an IT firm that offers a maintenance plan to have them do the work for you.

- *Perform an audit of your systems to document them for insurance and DR purposes,* as well as determine their current "health and security" status. Again, this may be a document readily available from an IT provider that maintains your network. If you wish to perform these audits on your own, a SIMPLE scan of each machine with BELARC Advisor (***www.belarc.com***) may give you some documentation to fall back on; however, a quality IT provider can offer you a more extensive audit as well as determine if your systems are healthy, need updates or require major fixes.

- *Install a backup solution for your data OR, for greater protection, consider a FULL IMAGE BACKUP of your machines.*

- Acquire a backup that uses drives, not tapes, and has an automated factor to it to remove the dependency on human interaction for its success.

- Your data is critical, consider frequent daily backups

- Your data is critical, consider a backup that can be redundantly stored offsite and virtualized locally or in the "Cloud." It should be encrypted to make it secure and more resilient to cyber-attacks like *CryptoWall*.

- To envision how critical it is, imagine your office functioning without that application.

- If you have a special *Line-of-Business* application software, determine if a HOSTED version of the product is offered by the publisher to enable you to run it in "The Cloud" and have the data remotely accessible at all times, as well as automatically backed up and updated whenever the revisions change.

NOTE: This carries a *caveat* for subscribers inasmuch as the data you use is not necessarily available to you on the ground, nor is a copy readily available should you wish to part ways with the provider. ***Always ask the important questions BEFORE you sign on for such a service.***

- *Consider using hosted Email* with good technical support to reduce your system's complexity and enhance reliability and extensibility of your messaging system. The initial cost is far lower to use than an outright purchase of a mail server (Exchange) for your office. Depending on your company's size, you might opt for the local server; however, the hosted one will offload cost as well as enable you to write off the service as an operational rather than capital expense.

NOTE: Any time a **HOSTED** service becomes a critical component in your daily production process, the need for Internet access rises in priority. As a measure to maintain a consistent level of access to the Internet, we strongly urge you to implement a **HIGH AVAILABILITY** (HA) measure and establish a failover **INTERNET SERVICE PROVIDER** (ISP) service to use in the event a backhoe or other interruption affects a specific provider. If you have no power on premises, it will not matter which ISP you are using, your computers will be down. To prepare for a power outage, budget for a *standalone power generator* to run (automatically) and maintain a clean, stable source of electricity for your machines. Remember to account for air conditioning in hot weather situations, as well.

Test your systems with "Fire Drills" – the same way your children practice for a fire at their schools, it is prudent to declare an emergency to your staff so you may practice your DR Plan and see what works and what does not. You might want to go *offsite*. **Only practice makes perfect.**

The Fire Drill

The fire drill is a very important part of our company's duty as an employer to ensure that all you, as staff, know how to react in the event of a fire. At least one drill will be held every 6 months by law. This can either be pre-planned and let everyone know there is going to be a drill at a certain time and a certain place or the more effective way would be to have a completely unannounced drill.

The purpose of the fire drill is to:

• Ensure that you, as staff, know the correct procedure to follow in case of a fire.

• To ensure persons nominated as Fire Marshalls carry out their duties effectively.

• To underpin staff training.

• To help identify any problems with the emergency plan.

Note that the process is **PLAN, BRIEF, EXECUTE, DEBRIEF.** By testing to see if the process works, it can be verified or refined, thus becoming a dependable plan to implement when needed. The same holds true for a Disaster Recovery Plan.

Business Continuity

The concept of Business Continuity can be envisioned in a multifaceted level. To truly get a feel for what it entails, we have broken it out into multiple phases. This is not to be construed as the complete list, merely a foundational outline to help you understand how encompassing this process is.

A Business Continuity Plan (BCP) takes the questions you ask after an "event" and extends it into documentation to outline what you must do to, not only recover from a disaster of varied extents, but establish a healthy guide to recover and stabilize post-event for all variations. In a way, it is a superset of the steps followed in a Disaster Recovery scenario.

The Small Business Development Center of NJ (SBDCNJ) offers insight sessions to its members. We recently attended one on Business Continuity—here is an excerpt from their handout.

Could you survive another disaster?

IMAGINE: Your building has been totally destroyed, you didn't get anything out and you can't get back in. The reasons do not matter.

ITEMS TO CONSIDER:

1. How long would it take to replace your building (or relocate), replace your critical equipment and reopen?

2. With your building destroyed, your income stopped and given your answer to #1, how long would you survive with the funds you have now?

3. Do you know what insurance(s) you have and are they enough to restart your business? How long would it take for you to get those funds?

4. Do you have pictures of your current facility, a complete inventory of equipment and copies of your insurance policies stored off site to facilitate your claims for damages?

5. Do you have names and contact information for the parties needed to rebuild your facility, replace your equipment and restart your business?

6. Do you have a way to inform your customers and others who need to know what happened and what do you tell them?

7. What legal documents, vital records and special forms do you need to operate your business and how soon could you have them replaced if destroyed?

8. Do you have backups of your PC data stored offsite, how long would it take to get new hardware and do you know how to restore your data on new hardware?

9. Do you have a written plan for how to recover from this or other disasters?

10. Where do you go for help?

These questions are designed to spark your interest and inspire the awareness of what needs to be reviewed PRIOR to any event occurring.

We will now delve into some of the aspects of Business Continuity that will help you deliver longevity to your organization.

As you examine your business to respond to the aforementioned questions, we want you to also to consider another aspect of each question postulated:
- **S**trength:
- **W**eakness:
- **O**pportunity
- **T**hreat

If you can apply a ***SWOT Analysis*** to each situation, you will find you develop better insight as to how you may address them. Keep in mind if you have a *hurricane*, you should also consider the threat of a *power outage* and *flooding*, which requires more in terms of planning and knowing how to work around the situation.

Some examples of SWOT are:

A Forecast Hurricane	
Strength	You know it's coming.
Weakness	You cannot control the situation.
Opportunity	Make certain that your offsite backup is functional and current.
Threat	Trees may block the road to your office.

A Natural Gas Leak	
Strength	You can smell the methane odor.
Weakness	You cannot safely address the situation and must contact emergency services.
Opportunity	Take your equipment with you off premise in case the gas ignites.
Threat	Your office may catch fire or explode.

Each SWOT may add a "Special Threat" such as flooding compounded with a hurricane. It pays to prepare; by spending the extra moments to extend your thoughts on how to survive an oncoming challenge.

Think back to Hurricane Katrina. If you recall, the storm was initially expected to make landfall in a sparsely populated area in Florida. Instead, the storm took a turn for the worse and hit New Orleans. The results were devastating. Had the Federal Emergency Management Agency (FEMA) been able to do more to prepare, do you think the outcome would have been different?

This is why we work on SWOT Analysis tables.

Operations Continuity

Every business must examine its risk. **Business Risk Management** is defined as *"the art and science of dealing with business uncertainty and its effects on operations."* It should be proactive, integrated and preventative.

There are six (6) processes that comprise Business Risk Management:

1. Plan Risk Management
2. Identify Risks
3. Perform Qualitative Risk Analysis
4. Perform Quantitative Risk Analysis
5. Plan Risk Responses
6. Control Risks

As you work through your day, you need to identify all aspects of your daily tasks. Try to write them down as you determine each aspect of your tasks.

If, for example, you are a personnel manager, do you run credit checks, workers comp claim checks or background checks on your candidates? Is their permission incorporated into whatever forms you provide them with to apply for work with you? Do you have others in the organization interview them to affirm your inclinations? Does the hiring manager take an active role in the interview process? Do the future colleagues partake in the process, as well?

Each role that you play, each task that you perform, every day that you work, try to observe and record what you do. Down the road, this will not only help you, but make your life easier.

Maybe, all you need is an employment manual for everybody. Until you begin the process of self-evaluation, you might not realize how much you accomplish every day or how many roles you fulfill on a regular basis. This will not only help you to create a job definition for future positions, but will slowly and methodically enable you to grow your organization as you plan for its continual improvement and future.

A business continuity plan does not only have to do with disasters, but should be a game plan for your business. If you have not done so at this point, we strongly suggest that you begin drafting a **BUSINESS PLAN** on 'paper' so you have a document to follow and guide you through your changes.

There are many things to consider when your business is in a DR mode or running its business continuity drills. As incredible as it may sound, many offices tend to overlook a glaring resource that, if not included in the process, will break the entire result: **_your employees_**.

Below, we will present you with a number of questions you should be asking to help prepare for any level of "event." The important concept to grasp is that each question is the foundation to building a set of procedures to outline and document the steps and phases of your continuity plan. Try to envision them as you ask these questions to yourself **_out loud_** and as you formulate additional ideas going along. Now is a good time to have a pen and paper handy to begin your vision.

Imagine a fire or a flood hits your office.

- Do you have a printed escape route in a conspicuous location in your office to indicate all exits?

- Do you have a list of all employees that were onsite that day? Do you have a way to track daily attendance onsite?

- Can you account for all of them once everyone has evacuated the building?

- What if the fire occurs at night and no one is there?

- How will you contact them in the morning to alert them to the fact that the office is no longer available and that they may need to work from their homes or an alternate location?

- Do you have the **personal contact numbers** for your managers and do they have the numbers for their subordinates and other personnel?

- Do each of your **key personnel** have a *backup person* who can perform their critical function in the event they are cut off or incapacitated by the event?

- Have you pre-arranged for all critical employees to have (**remote**) **access** to an **alternate location** from which to conduct business in the event your office is inaccessible?

- Do they have **Voice over IP (VoIP) phones** that give a professional presence when they call? If not, how long would it take to get them to your staff?

- Do they have a **hosted email Server** (in the "Cloud") from which they may send emails and give the client the peace of mind in knowing that they are still being supported?

- Do you have some way to track the work being performed by your employees so they may be duly compensated for their work?

- Have you drafted a copy of a **list of all critical clients and vendors** in order to maintain a continuous relationship with them? *Can you access it or do you have it with you?*

- Do you have **emergency business checks** and access to a recent, if not current, copy of **your company's financial software** in order to bill and pay outstanding invoices?

- Do you have copies of all needed business software applications and their **product keys/licenses** in order to document your legitimate right to continue using them?

- Do you have a hard copy or additional electronic copy of your **company's insurance policies** and **employee handbook** with a designated Human Resources contact?

- Have you determined all of the needed **team leaders** to successfully restore your company to its functional level?

- Do you have designated **teams** and **team leaders** assigned within your organization who fully understand their responsibilities as stated in the Business Continuity Plan?

As you can see, planning for the unexpected can involve tedious levels of forethought. You may think of most circumstances that may arise, but it is not unlikely that there will be once aspect that you will overlook. Hopefully, the time you spend anticipating in any type of event will never need to be implemented. This may sound like an exercise in futility, but in the long run, it's worth it.

Now, as you review the breakout sections below, try to identify the simple process that you can apply to create your own outline from the questions provided and those that you think of as you review the items shown. Remember, every business will have similar and unique needs from those provided. You will need to identify the questions and circumstances that apply to your situation and generate the procedures that will work for you should you require the activation of a business continuity plan.

To help you keep your ideas in a central location, we have provided a section at the end of this book for you to keep notes. Good luck and congratulations on your step forward.

To help motivate you in the process, keep in mind that Business Continuity Planning (BCP) will help you to reduce the impact of business interruption, minimize risk, protect the business, employees and the community, improve products and services, develop preparedness and response strategies, keep you current on rules and regulations, build a competitive advantage and improve you public image—all worthwhile benefits for your effort.

Technology & Data Management

Technology tends to reflect Business Continuity in its plans more than most aspects of the business. It is inherently needed by a business due to the heavy dependency of data and the randomness of failures within this aspect.

Hard drives have long been gauged to last about 100,000 hours as their *Mean Time Between Failures* (MTBF) rating. If you were to convert that value into days or months or years, you would find it is equivalent to about 11 years, 23 weeks, 1 day and 16 hours. Given an expected lifetime for a hard drive, you might anticipate having your equipment around for more than 4-5 years on average; however, in reality, most computers in a commercial environment have an expectancy of about 5 years. This is attributable to the fact that technology changes and the needs of the business adjust accordingly.

So, what does a business do to maintain itself in light of an emergency event such as a storm, flood, fire or sabotage?

Most people would say maintain a backup. The follow-up question to ask, however, is what type of backup will you run? There are **USB drives**, **tapes**, **network attached storage** (NAS) devices and other media available for backups. There are **Full Image** and **File & Folder** backups. Then, there is the rotation of tapes or retention period for which you must retain the copies. Do you keep them onsite in a fireproof safe or do you store them offsite through a service like Iron Mountain or automatically have them stored offsite in redundant dual coast locations like Datto? Do you allow your data to be stored by the lowest cost provider that may store it in an offshore location such as India or England or do you require your provider to maintain storage within the domestic United States to maintain compliance with federal regulations and laws?

You need to review your industry's written standards if they exist or consult with a professional to determine which solution would work best for you.

Many residential users may use *Carbonite*, *Mozy* or *iBackup* to protect their personal files and photos. You need to determine if these are solutions that work for you or not. Not all **File & Folder** backups will recover at the same speed. Keep in mind that if you are able to retain a local copy on an external drive, you should be able to access it quicker than the person that is forced to download the same amount of data over the Internet. Don't lose track of the fact that a 65GB download of your data may take from a few hours to a few days, whereas, the same data could be moved locally from an external drive to a computer's (local) drive much faster. Oh, yes, and remember that the local *external* drive may be lost under the same circumstances as your computers.

An alternate to *File & Folder* is **Full Image**. There are a number of software applications on the market that enable a user to run a backup with a full image. We have used *Acronis*, *Appassure*, *Veritas* and *StorageCraft*, but clearly have found our preference to be with *StorageCraft ShadowProtect*. The beauty of using a full image backup is the fact that you are able to restore the full machine in one single pass. When you restore a machine using File &

Folder, you must first restore the operating system, then you run a utility to restore the files and folders. If you are using a server, it is complicated to do the restore inasmuch as the entire security structure may need to be restored in stages.

So, you have addressed the backup, what about your network and Internet? How do you propose to reinstate your access to that?

Many businesses have found that they are able to maintain a secondary connection to the Internet via a cellular network (MiFi) implementation. This is a valid *temporary* solution—particularly because it is slow. An option that you should also consider is sharing space.

Whenever a business is in recovery mode of Business Continuity or going through their Disaster Recovery process, having a shared space with a compatible colleague can be a game changer. By sharing space and a network, you are often able to regain much of your competitive edge by being able to send out emails and other missives. Furthermore, having a network can also enable you to run your Voice over IP (VoIP) phones and regain a customer service component. Too many businesses lose power and do not consider moving to their homes or a temporary business location. They simply look at their old venue and say, "I can't wait until we get power again." *You must always be **two** steps ahead in your planning to avert an emergency.* Have a plan, test it, work it and once you feel good about it, fully document the plan and make sure that everyone involved in executing it has a full copy with complete lists of contacts and their anticipated locations.

Your business may have some level of flexibility if you have implemented a hosted website, hosted Exchange email server or have your data and applications in the "Cloud." Even if you don't have a desktop, if you can get your hand on a simple computer that gets Internet, you can open your email in a web browser and respond to your clients and help them know that you are there for them.

An important aspect of running your server in the cloud is that your personnel are able to do a dry run or test its viability at any time and from any place, effectively establishing a full blown verification of the system in the event of an emergency.

One added step that you must always consider is making arrangements for your cloud to be backed up. Read your online service agreement carefully and confirm that it assures you of a backup performed daily or with greater frequency from one server to another in a redundant location. For those of you that do not have this in their agreement, we strongly suggest having that conversation with your IT Service Provider.

They can either setup your system to have an alternate location prepared with a duplicating software application such as "**DoubleTake**" from Sunbelt Software, establish a backup using **Backupify** (Cloud-to-Cloud Backup) from Datto. A program like this is valuable because it will not only service your proprietary setup, but can be used to back up your data if you are using *Microsoft Office365*, *Google Apps* and *Salesforce*. It is a solution for those using ***Software-As-A-Service*** (SaaS).

Recovery Teams & Crisis Management

Anticipating a disaster is always a challenge. That is why having a team of employees work together improves your odds of having greater success surviving an event of any magnitude.

For those of you that are fans of the US TV program, The Office, you may be familiar with the episode in which Dwight stages a Fire Drill which causes a panic and an employee has a heart attack as a result of the tumult and chaos. Obviously, this is the opposite of your objective.

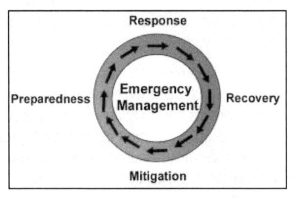

Establishing a Recovery Team & Crisis Management committee in your organization has the singular purpose of helping you to coordinate a safe and orderly recovery from any mishap that may come your way. Please understand that a mishap is not limited to a fire or flood, it could represent a breach of information, a legal issue, a human resources issue, a safety issue or a power outage. It is only limited by what fate can throw your way.

It may shock you to consider this, but if the "event" that affects your organization should be a data breach, have you ever given it thought regarding who you might want to contact first to get your "bases covered"? Many would initially respond, I would call the cops, your IT provider or the insurance company; however, if you consider the circumstances and the ramifications of your actions, it may actually be most effective for you to contact your lawyer. That's correct.

Consider the following scenario:

Your company's computer system has just been breached. You have an insurance policy that is available to cover you if such an occurrence happened, so you call the insurance company. The insurance company starts their process and calls your IT provider and/or an IT forensic expert. They then contact a legal expert to address your other concerns. If you were summoned into court to testify on what happened, the IT forensics expert may be subpoenaed, too. Since he or she works for the insurance company, they may be required to provide an affidavit of their findings. Any results found are now revealed to government agencies for potential fines or actions under a myriad of laws or regulations and details are also available for lawsuits from affected clients or consumers.

Now, envision having contacted the lawyer first.

The lawyer contacts the insurance company, the IT forensics expert et al. HOWEVER, the reports were arranged by YOUR LAWYER. Inasmuch as the lawyer did this on your behalf, the reports are now subject to *Attorney/Client Privilege* protection and will not be easily released during any discovery process since they are protected. We urge you to discuss this with counsel to validate this, but in a conversation with Steven S. Rubin, Esq. of *Moritt Hock & Hamroff,* we were strongly swayed to understand this as accurate.

Mr. Rubin recommends a **WISP** (Written Information Security Plan) be in place to protect the company and its assets. The WISP "sets forth the company's methodologies in identifying, protecting, detecting and responding to incidents and creates a network of relationships with experts to contact in the event of a suspected breach." (Rubin, 2015)

As cited, for some steps in a plan, it is critical that they are given significant forethought. By engaging your support structure to follow a prescribed and sequenced process, you may afford your organization added protections that may have been surrendered otherwise.

Not only would your Recovery Teams and Crisis Management contacts help you on a legal front, but they should also be engaged to help you to identify contingency locations or establish interoffice alliances with either colleagues in the business or with totally unrelated businesses with the objective of sharing space under special agreements and terms to be effective when your facility or their facilities may be compromised by weather, politics, police action or any other circumstance that either keeps your or them away from their offices.

The Team should provide step-by-step instructions on how-to execute any phase of the BCP and who should do it. They should also list the roles and have them listed with the names of those given each responsibility. The more details provided, the clearer the instruction and greater the compliance.

Risk Management

Although many understand what RISK represents, not everyone knows how to plan for it and take evasive measures to avoid the pain of a bad risk. Risk Management represents a cyclical process that can be summed up in four phases:

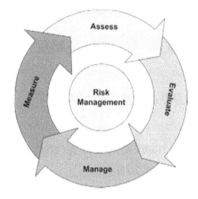

Assess: Consider the possible concerns posed by a situation and list them out for further scrutiny. Do this for as many scenarios as you can imagine relative to your business.

Evaluate: Review each of the concerns listed in the *Assess* phase to determine where it lies on the priority scale. Sort the concerns by priority in descending order.

Manage: Review the concerns by priority and examine how your business may respond to them. Consider as many options as you can, then develop written plans to address them.

Measure: Determine the impact that each managed concern amounts to, calculate its overall impact on your business, then repeat the Assess phase with this new insight.

Risks exist in all aspects of a business. Ask yourself some questions to highlight some risks, then focus on the key aspects of the question to work on its risk analysis component for risk management. Here are some sample

"**What if...**" questions you may ask pertaining to your company...

- *What if a key employee decides to go to a competitor?*

- *What if a virus affects our computer network?*

- *What if we miss an important deadline in a contracted agreement?*

- *What if a tree falls on our facility and injures one of our employees?*

- *What if we miss an important payment on a leased piece of equipment?*

- *What if the single bridge on the road leading to our building is washed away during a storm?*

- *What if the inventory in our warehouse is flooded during a storm?*

I think you get the point by now. As you can understand, doing a Risk Analysis on any aspect of your business will lead you to important revelations in weaknesses. At the same time, if you consider each one carefully, you can actually perform a SWOT analysis and turn them from losses to gains. Let's take one example and break it out using the Risk Management cycle.

What if a key employee decides to go to a competitor?

Although this may not be an emergency in some eye's it still represents a vulnerability that must be addressed.

Concerns posed by this change may include: (ASSESS)

- Key employee moving to a competitor may result in lost business or productivity due to one less person on team.

- Movement of employee from organization means certain workflow knowledge and trade secrets may be lost.

- If employee had extensive relationships with external contacts at client offices, this may pull them away from us.

- Now we must replace a worker by either promoting from within or recruiting a new employee.

- If person was strong leader, others may follow in search of better wages, benefits, leadership or location.

These evaluative items are now randomly listed. Perhaps, we can list them by priority so we may begin to manage them better. In the big picture, you will want to consider both the short term and long term effects of this event. After passing it through the cycle a second time, your opinion my need to be revised. (EVALUATE)

1. If employee had extensive relationships with external contacts at client offices, this may pull them away from us.

2. Movement of employee from organization means certain workflow knowledge and trade secrets may be lost.

3. Now we must replace a worker by either promoting from within or recruiting a new employee.

4. Key employee moving to a competitor may result in lost business or productivity due to one less person on team.

5. If person was strong leader, others may follow in search of better wages, benefits, leadership or location.

Now that you have listed the concerns in priority order, let's see how we can manage each one separately which resulted from this situation.

If employee had extensive relationships with external contacts at our clients' offices, this may draw them away from us.

(MANAGE)

1. Your business should have an **EMPLOYEE HANDBOOK** which lists clear guidelines by which they are employed and expected to behave.

2. It should be clearly stated that any employee may **NOT SOLICIT** current clients for a minimum of one year post-employment from company, regardless of basis for departure.

3. You should review the departing employee's quarterly or annual reviews to determine whether a pattern had developed over time to show a lack of interest of drop in reviewed productivity or attitude.

4. If you did not rate employee poorly, determine if any recognition was offered to that person either in the form of financial or other benefit.

5. If that person always performed as a key employee, was any bonus awarded during the year?

6. Have you recently reviewed your offering packages to determine whether they are competitive with the current market?

7. Can you determine if the departing employee has accessed, copied or removed any critical documents that would be considered theft? **Before any measures are taken**, request that this person return all company property and sign an affidavit to attest to the the fact that no other copies or items are in their possession. Confirm that this person complies.

8. Review your sales procedures and make certain that there are procedures to provide for oversight of all communications between sales personnel and managers.

9. If this person worked in a smaller company and reported to you, verify that you did your due diligence in this matter.

10. Upon the departure of said employee, did you notify the clients that this person was no longer under your employ? *What have you done for them lately to generate loyalty?*

You have now reviewed the one concern and now you have TEN. Do you feel you did a complete assessment of this MANAGEMENT ISSUE? If so, let's move onto the final phase of MEASURE.

The Measurement phase might not be as straightforward to complete in a brief period of time. Remember, you do

NOT know if this person has removed any competitively valued data nor do you know if they are intent on "stealing" your clients, so you must now examine your details that are pertinent to the ex-employee.

(MEASURE)

Your business has been around for a decade and has about 100 steady clients and 200 infrequent ones. You must now identify the clients that had direct involvement with the former employee and note from the time this person began with you up to the two to four weeks prior to disengagement, how much you can ascertain your organization made from each client that they knew and what the numbers were. You will need to monitor these numbers carefully. Try to determine if you see any pattern change in their spending habits. Are any of them now reducing their transactions or transactional value? Can you determine if it is due to changes in their status or possibly due to "another" factor? Any changes that you can document and prove MAY be viable for a breach of contract. Otherwise, it may be time to review your business practices and see where refinements should occur.

Now, you should repeat the ASSESS phase and perform those refinements.

You have now seen a simple example of what it takes to analytically assess and refine your business for both a Business Continuity Plan and for a general Business Plan. Either way, we hope that these examples have been germane and pertinent to your organization.

Communication Planning

Establishing a hierarchical path for communications is what this is about. When a fire may occur in the building where you work, how are people notified of this emergency situation? It's simple, you make arrangements to establish automated and semi-automated modes to advise your employees and clients through prepared and common channels. In other words, as soon as a fire is detected (by smoke detectors or seen by a person), either an alarm is pulled or the detector triggers an alarm. That is the first level of communications. Once it goes off, you may also make a public announcement over a public address (PA) system to announce a fire has been detected on the second floor, please evacuate the building immediately using the staircase on the north side because the south side is overcome by smoke. You may also have a 911 button or setting that notifies the emergency services (e.g., fire and rescue). As a third level of contact, your company (depending on size) may have a telephone call tree where #1 calls #2, #2 calls #3, #3 calls #4 and so forth. Additional notices may be setup on a Central Call in phone number for all employees and/or you may also post an emergency notice on the company's website's homepage or announce status face-to-face.

Whatever options you choose to employ, you cannot have too many options. In a scenario with an approaching storm, you may use a modified method to communicate ADVISORIES, WATCHES, WARNINGS and ALERTS via company emails, pages or text messages. If no advanced warning is received, you might follow similar channels as used for a local fire. If the storm is upon you and you have properly prepared and drilled for such a threat, then you may also have to determine whether or not the personnel will need to be evacuated or sheltered-in-place. If **Shelter-In-Place** (S-I-P) is a strong likelihood, then you should also have prepared by storing emergency food and provisions to support any expected number of staff for a short term.

If your business were situated in hurricane or tornado alley, then your plan would need to be well documented with maps, full instructions, and an *Emergency Coordinator* (EC) (and secondary EC) to make certain all plans are implemented in a calm and orderly fashion as tested. *In such situations, confusion is your enemy*, so you will have to know exactly who and how many people are present to account for all onsite. Such details would need to be explicitly documented in your plans to assure no step is missed or procedure overlooked.

Make certain to communicate clearly the first time and every time!

Employee & Human Capital Planning

If your business is small, you may need to use all of your staff in the event of an emergency; however, a larger organization may be able to furlough some staff for the sake of continuity. As your business develops its plans, it may realize that there are critical staff that perform functions necessary on a daily basis and there are others that are not as pressing. For some companies, creating this portion of their BCP may lead them to identify staff that they do not require even on a regular basis, thus a potential reduction in force may occur prior to any incident.

For every person participating in your BCP, you must have all of their contact information. You should prepare a list of Key Stakeholders, their home address and phone, cellular phone, office phone and business/personal email addresses to facilitate all possible modes of contact. Once you have them listed, establish a phone chain for them to follow in the event an emergency is declared.

Keep in mind, there may be personnel in your office that will be activated for other purposes (e.g., National Guard, Fire, Auxiliary Police, EMS, jury duty, out-of-town on business or vacation), so their presence might be changed given certain circumstances. Have alternates for all members whenever possible. For all participants, similar to the chain, make sure to delegate authority to the appropriate parties and enable them to make decisions as the company for their role. This is not to remove power from those that normally wield it, but to enable action when action is needed and communications are poor at best. Make it clear that their determination to act should be based on a "Must Do" or "Need to Do" priority, not "Could Do." As long as these folks are who you think they are, they should act in a responsible fashion and not need to be second-guessed. Your list should be as large as necessary, but as small as possible.

Consider not just the high ranking members of your management staff, but review those that do low to mid-level jobs, as well. An accounts receivable clerk who tracks your incoming payments and makes sure that all clients are current is a valid example of such a person.

While you are planning for these people to be accessible, you should also consider how they will be available. If you have an office in the City, will you put them up in a hotel? Will you provide them with car service to get to the office without having to park when it might not be available? Are you planning to feed them to help them stay at the location? Will you need to dispatch them to other locations? All of these questions must be considered because you are trying to anticipate your future needs while you may be under duress. It's time to put all the pieces of the people puzzle together.

Supply Chain Continuity

A disaster has been declared, but it could be by you or your supplier. Have you given additional thought to the prospect of your vendor closing their doors? Your plans must always provide a contingency for not only your inconvenience of being displaced, but must also address the potential for the vendors on your list being displaced or closed as well.

Have a list in your Ready Kit that will provide all names of all vendors and all lists of items they sell to you at recent pricing. You should be able to use a list like this to either resume where you left off or negotiate pricing with a new vendor in a comparable manner should you no longer be able to conduct business with the prior (incumbent) vendor.

What about if you have an inventory in your building and the facility is to be closed for a planned period to make alterations? Do you have the resources to move the items to a storage facility nearby so you may continue to access the items? Could you lease vehicles or trucks for your sales force or delivery staff to work without interruption?

In the event of an emergency, not everyone should be able to sign on behalf of the company, but what if no one has been granted authority to act on the organization's behalf and the key personnel that could are unavailable. Have agreements in place to enable the critical personnel to act on the company's behalf. It should be as simple as creating a template for each vendor, listing alternates and sending it to them by an authorized party PRIOR to any need emerging. Remember, you are planning to be viable after an event, so you must prepare for it now.

Safety, Testing & Maintenance

Whether you are in a service industry or manufacturing, you must be sure to have safety measures in place. It could be as simple as a map on the wall with labeled escape routes and exit signs at the doors. For others, it may be having an eye wash station to address a common hazard in the workplace. In any situation, there are steps you must consider, evaluate and post in your workplace to assure the safety of your workers.

If you are in an office with a person using the phone extensively, it may be the expectation that a headset would be provided to avoid a neck injury due to a repetitive stress disorder. You know your environment and the hazards that you potentially face on a regular basis. It is up to you, as management, to provide the area conducive to conducting business in a healthy and non-hostile manner.

Speaking of hostile, if your employees have Internet access, do you provide a business-class router that offers a Content Filtering Service (CFS) to keep out questionable content from viewer's screens? It does not matter if it is a house of worship or a busy accounting office, if one of your employees views an image on a screen that has been accessed over the Internet and it is considered "offensive" to them, you may have a safety issue (not to mention a hostile work environment lawsuit) to contend with. The potential for creating a safe environment is up to you based upon your knowledge. If you feel you are ignorant or short on ideas, consider engaging a consultant to help you assess your situation.

Testing and Maintenance generally reflect your organization performing due diligence to assure all safety measures work and are kept functional. If you have a smoke detector, do you perform fire drills or depress the test button on occasion? Have you installed a hard wired or battery-operated device? Do you replace the batteries every 4 to 6 months to be sure it works? These are simple examples of Testing and Maintenance.

In the example above regarding a CFS, did your IT Administrator test the router to make certain the Content Filtering was setup properly and filters out only the subjects that you wish to block. If you were to run a pharmacy, you might not want "Drugs" blocked, but if you have a house of worship, you would want "Pornographic," "Negligee" or "Swimsuits" on the do not display list. It is all a question of what you do. Renewing and keeping it active would be considered due diligence for maintenance since CFS is a subscription-based service.

One of the most important considerations in today's world is testing and maintaining your office data backup. If you were to experience an interruption and you could not recover your data, the odds are against your business surviving past the next two years. Always have a backup performed daily or more often, test the backup and, if you need to replace media or renew a subscription for service, do not let it lapse. ***Your business clearly depends upon it.***

Years ago, businesses depended upon tapes to record their backups. Tapes were sensitive to electromagnetic sources, heat, cold and overuse. Too often, the person in charge of the backups would test the backup, but when the time came to do an actual restore, the most successful tapes could fail. The result of tests was that the tape ribbon became more susceptible to breakage. Can you imagine your mood when the tape that your whole business depended upon proved to be trash. It is not where you want to be.

In an effort to engage more reliable media, technicians now install backups that use hard drives, Solid State Drives (SSDs), Network Attached Storage (NAS) appliances and cloud storage. This has proven to be significantly more reliable and dependable. If you are still using tapes, we strongly urge you to evaluate your current backup recovery system.

By migrating to a newer systems, you not only can remove the human aspect from the equation, but can get a system that takes NO VACATIONS, DOES NOT REQUIRE A SECONDARY PERSON, EXPECTS NO BONUS OR HEALTH BENEFITS, is fully automated, backs up to reliable media using an appliance that can process backups every 15 minutes, automatically transfers all copies to the cloud for offsite, at redundant locations with full encryption and regulatory compliance at securely monitored bicoastal venues and automatic screen verifications from virtual images to give you peace-of-mind on a regular basis.

Try to think of this section as a *workflow template* section. Your business needs to do `<blank>`. Knowing that it needs to be completed `<n>` times per `<period>`, you run it. To be sure it was completed, you do a `<test |review|audit>` of the results. If you have not run successfully, you must fix the job, it if does work right, you document and repeat the process.

Another aspect to the recovery scenario is a dependency upon having your phones working and having power available to keep your systems functional. Ever since the impact of Superstorm Sandy, the residents of the New York Metropolitan area have been keenly aware of their dependency upon electricity. Whether you need it to run your refrigerator, computer or burglar alarm, they depend upon a constant flow of energy to keep them functional.

The same can be said for your business. Your computers, servers, printers, copiers, fax machines, phones and other equipment would not server as more than a door stop without power to keep them running. For this reason, many businesses (and residences) have made the investment in their own dedicated generators. Before you invest in a generator, makes sure you consult with a licensed electrician and/or engineer who can properly determine your draw and overall usage. Some people have bought and incorrectly operated gas-powered generators and suffered from carbon monoxide poisoning. Don't become a statistic. Do your due diligence and get it done properly—even if it costs a little more—in the long run, you will be glad you did.

Finally, test your phones. If you have a Private Branch Exchange (PBX) phone system installed in your office, make sure it is able to reroute calls in the event of a power outage. If you use Voice over IP (VoIP) phones, they run on the same network as your computers, so you will need to keep power fed to your network. In the case of an outage, however, many HOSTED PBX systems will automatically route to the phone wherever it is, so if the desk set is in another location, it does not matter. Give them a test and be ready.

Assessing both Economic & Physical Injury

It's time to pre-assess the impact of an interruption or disaster in terms of how it may hit your business **economically**...

- How much did we lose not being able to service our clients?

- How many clients did we lose as a result of our interruption?

- How long will it take for us to return to a profitable level?

- How long will it take us to setup the business in a new location that is convenient to our client-base?

- Did our state of preparedness (good or bad) help or hinder us in terms of conducting future business with our clients?

- As a result of the interruption, did we breach any of our contractual obligations? Can the matters be remediated?

- Did we have adequate business interruption insurance to help us recover from the events at hand?

Remember to ask yourself questions like the ones shown above to help you formulate a plan to clearly determine the economic impact any "event" may have upon your business. Do not forget to examine the peripheral impact, as well, loss of "good will". Often, you may have had an interruption and recovered, but your clients may see it as a negative experience in doing business with your organization and, aside from not continuing to transact business with you, may share their experiences with other prospects that ask them for an opinion about your company. It is not a source of libel or slander, it is just them sharing their honest opinion and personal experience. That, too, may harm you.

Try to envision the multiple scenarios and anticipate what you will have to contend with in terms of a **_SWOT Analysis_**. For example, if you need to acquire business interruption insurance, it is something you must do beforehand. Don't wait for a hurricane warning before you attempt to get flood coverage. You are unlikely to get it if they see the same risk that you see.

In addition to the economic impact, you must also acknowledge the **physical injury** it has on your company…

- Was anyone injured during the event and is now processing a workers' compensation or other lawsuit?

- Were any of the key players in the organization injured, lost or unavailable as a result of the situation? If so, how will we recover their contribution to the business' bottom line?

- Did you have key players insurance to cover an employee or manager's exit from the company whether attributable to an incident, death, accident or "moving on"?

- Were any company trade secrets lost as a result of the recent event? Do we have the information stored elsewhere?

- How much of your equipment and facility will be able to be recovered or repurposed in your recovery process?

Just as you would do to prepare for the economic impact, you must do for the physical impact. Knowing that a key player has been looking and now found a job is not the right time to ask them to sign a non-disclosure or non-compete agreement. Use your progressive thought to envision each step and the next step that would occur in as many processes as you can.

Preparation is the bottom line to your business success, particularly in terms of operations and management. If you need assistance in determining your best path to take, deliberation may be part of your processing, but in such instances, it can have traumatic results. Business Continuity Planning cannot tolerate the mantra, "Why put off till tomorrow what you can put off till the day after tomorrow?" If that is you, then get yourself help from an outside company that can provide you with the services to focus on these matters. Be a proactive entrepreneur, not a reactive firefighter.

Are you REALLY covered?
Insurance Considerations.

Recent advertisements on the TV have portrayed insurance salesmen talking to their clients/prospects about what they are paying for and what is actually covered by their policies. If you have not recently reviewed your insurance policies for your business to confirm that you are getting what you pay for, it is time to schedule that appointment.

Many businesses may have insurance to cover their business in the event of a fire, flood or theft; however, they may not have **cyber insurance** to protect them in the event their business is involved in a breach, data corruption, sabotage or, simply put, something they had not anticipated. Unless you have verified it, you may be located in a flood plain and, although you did request it, are not covered for flood insurance because the insurer would not provide it to you based on your risk level (and presumed you would have reviewed the policy before signing up and paying for it). **Does this describe you?**

Of course, not all insurance used in business is technology related, but many of the policies are now inclusive or additive to address the new source of potential threats and risks inherent with doing business online.

Some insurers may offer your company a discount if you can document that all of your employees have gone through training in spotting a phishing scam or how to avoid getting a virus. If the training was completed and documented, you may be able to submit it for a reduction in your policy. Think of it as the "Good Student Discount" that you got for automobile insurance when you sent in a copy of your child's report card with a 3.0 or better average. They could call it the "Human Firewall" benefit.

As mentioned earlier, it often boils down to the inherent risk borne by them for insuring a company that has a website for potential liability, stores Personally Identifiable Information (PII) that holds potential for breach leading to fraud and theft, or maintaining confidentiality, again, a breach risk with any number of downsides.

If you are able to demonstrate that you have implemented the necessary precautions to reduce or eliminate the downsides, you may qualify for discounts— ask your insurer if they are available or if your policies offer them.

The Physical Aspect

We've discussed the intangible aspects of the business, but you must also review your policies to see if you will receive coverage for instances of replacing your office components:

- Computers, Printers, Copiers
- Desks, Cabinets, and other furniture
- Cabling for phones and data
- Carpeting, wood flooring and other facility concerns
- Business Interruption Coverage during the recovery
- Incidentals needed to recover/continue post-events
- Lost Inventory and stock items

One major document should also be available— photographs of each item that you wish to replace, including the facility's full views of the building and work environment.

Sample Business "Ready Kit"

The New Jersey Small Business Development Center (NJSBDC) has drafted an excellent selection of items to include in your kit and how to assemble it. [Pamphlet: "**Ready for Anything**: *Plan to Stay in Business"*, NJSBDC Network] Keep in mind, this is a template and you are welcome to add or remove from it as you deem best for your organization.

Ready Kit

Every business should have a "Ready Kit" that includes important documents and supplies necessary for business to continue after a small or large interruption or disaster. Some suggested items include access to:

☐ Business Continuity Plan

- o Emergency contact list of employees and key customers/clients
- o List of suppliers and vendors
- o Insurance policies and agent information
- o Emergency Action Plan

☐ Inventory list and pictures

- ☐ Voice mail box number and remote password
- ☐ Back-up computer system/data files
- ☐ Pictures of business interior and exterior
- ☐ Video or photos of company assets
- ☐ List of current values of all inventory and assets
- ☐ Camera to document damage
- ☐ Legal documents
- ☐ Current financials
- ☐ Last 3 years tax returns
- ☐ Cash reserves
- ☐ Bank records including checking, savings, credit and debit cards, loans and letters of credit.

IMPORTANT CONSIDERATION

Store your **"Ready Kit"** in a fire resistant and waterproof box in a safe offsite location and/or an online secure "vault" service.

Contact the NJSBDC (*www.njsbdc.com*) because, through a special grant by the US Small Business Administration, businesses impacted by local disasters can now take advantage of prepaid business assistance in planning for recovery. You don't have to "go it alone."

In Conclusion...

I feel fortunate to work in the field of Information Technology (IT) and be able to read and learn extensively about the latest in computers and networking. "Staying current" in my business is always challenging, but, at the same time, it is rewarding.

Having knowledge and not sharing it with others to benefit from is a trait of those lacking self-esteem and goodwill. It is my intent to share this knowledge to enable you to live a fuller life: one with less stress and greater gains. Whether you have learned more about Cybercrime, Disaster Recovery, Business Continuity or planning, your arrival at this point in the book represents a triumph for both of us over ignorance.

I want you to succeed and pay it forward. By maintaining a more stable business, you keep others employed, your community benefits from your contributions, and your life is better. How else can you help others?

Now that you are aware of the risks and how to avoid them, take the time to teach others, whether it is how to stay away from trouble by reducing your "attack surface" or not clicking on a questionable email message, or by buying copies of this book for all of your clients.

Everyone makes mistakes. If you or one of your clients has, we can provide corrective support. If you are interested in having us help you implement what you have learned in this book, we can do that, too! Finally, if you feel your business is "not there yet" and you want us to help you to assess and address your vulnerabilities, give us a call. We are dedicated to your success.

Glossary

Acceptable Use Policy — Also known as an **AUP**, is an agreement signed by all employees as a condition of employment. It is often a part of an Employee Handbook and provides an enforceable understanding with regard to the use of computers, telephones, faxes and Internet Access (amongst other things) in the office. This is often drafted or vetted by an attorney in order to assure it is valid in a court of law in the event an employee fails to abide by the terms stipulated and is either terminated or penalized.

One of its common uses is to warn employees that pornography, hate mongering sites and others that establish a hostile work environment will not be tolerated, nor will spamming and offensive acts of using corporate technology resources. It also establishes guidelines or prohibition of shopping and other personal activities.

BONUS: We are providing an **AUP template** in this book to get you started. ***Consult with legal counsel PRIOR to implementing it.***

To see the full article -
https://en.wikipedia.org/wiki/Acceptable_use_policy

Adware - (source: *Wikipedia*) or ***advertising-supported software***, is any software package that automatically renders advertisements in order to generate revenue for its author. The advertisements may be in the user interface of the software or on a screen presented to the user during the installation process. The functions may be designed to analyze which Internet sites the user visits and to present advertising pertinent to the types of goods or services featured there. The term is sometimes used to refer to software that displays unwanted advertisements.

To see the full article -
https://en.wikipedia.org/wiki/Adware

Antivirus - (source: *Wikipedia*) Also known as **"anti-virus"** software (often abbreviated as **AV**), sometimes known as **anti-malware** software, is computer software used to prevent, detect and remove malicious software.

To see the full article -
https://en.wikipedia.org/wiki/Antivirus_software

Backdoor- (source: *Wikipedia*) A **backdoor** in a computer system (or cryptosystem or algorithm) is a method of bypassing normal authentication, securing unauthorized remote access to a computer, obtaining access to plaintext, and so on, while attempting to remain undetected. The backdoor may take the form of a hidden part of a program, a separate program (e.g., Back Orifice) may subvert the system through a rootkit.

Default passwords can function as backdoors if they are not changed by the user. Some debugging features can also act as backdoors if they are not removed in the release version.

To see the full article -
https://en.wikipedia.org/wiki/Backdoor

BitCoin (BTC) – (source: *Wikipedia*) A payment system invented by *Satoshi Nakamoto*, who published the invention in 2008 and released it as open-source software in 2009. The system is peer-to-peer; users can transact directly without needing an intermediary. Transactions are  verified by network nodes and recorded in a public distributed ledger called the *block chain*. The ledger uses its own unit of account, also called *bitcoin*. The system works without a central repository or single administrator, which has led the US Treasury to categorize it as a *decentralized virtual currency.* Bitcoin is often called the first *cryptocurrency,* although prior systems existed. Bitcoin is more correctly described as the first *decentralized digital currency.* It is the largest of its kind in terms of total market value.

Bitcoins are created as a reward for payment processing work in which users offer their computing power to verify and record payments into the public ledger. This activity is called *mining* and is rewarded by transaction fees and newly created bitcoins. Besides mining, bitcoins can be obtained in exchange for different currencies, products, and services. Users can send and receive bitcoins for an optional transaction fee.

Bitcoin as a form of payment for products and services has grown, and merchants have an incentive to accept it because fees are lower than the 2–3% typically imposed by credit card processors. Unlike credit cards, any fees are paid by the purchaser, not the vendor. The European Banking Authority and other sources have warned that bitcoin users are not protected by refund rights or chargebacks. Despite a big increase in the number of merchants accepting bitcoin, the cryptocurrency doesn't have much momentum in retail transactions.

The use of bitcoin by criminals has attracted the attention of financial regulators, legislative bodies, law enforcement, and media. As of 2013, criminal activities primarily centered around theft and black markets. Officials in countries such as the United States also recognize that bitcoin can provide legitimate financial services.

To see the full article - *https://en.wikipedia.org/wiki/Bitcoin*

Blackhole exploit kit - (source: *Wikipedia*) is as of 2012 the most prevalent web threat, where 29% of all web threats detected by Sophos and 91% by AVG are due to this exploit kit. Its purpose is to deliver a malicious payload to a victim's computer. According to Trend Micro the majority of infections due to this exploit kit were done in a series of high volume spam runs. The kit incorporates tracking mechanisms so that people maintaining the kit know considerable information about the victims arriving at the kits landing page. The information tracked includes the victims country, operating system, browser and which piece of software on the victims computer was exploited. These details are shown in the kit's user interface.

To see the full article -
https://en.wikipedia.org/wiki/ Blackhole_exploit_kit

Botnet – (source: *Wikipedia*) is a number of Internet-connected computers communicating with other similar machines in an effort to complete repetitive tasks and objectives. This can be as mundane as keeping control of an Internet Relay Chat (IRC) channel, or it could be used to send spam email or participate in distributed denial-of-service attacks. The word *botnet* is a combination of the words *robot* and *network*. The term is usually used with a negative or malicious connotation.

To see the full article - *https://en.wikipedia.org/wiki/Botnet*

Computer Worm – (source: *Wikipedia*) A computer worm is a standalone malware computer program that replicates itself in order to spread to other computers. Often, it uses a computer network to spread itself, relying on security failures on the target computer to access it. Unlike a computer virus, it does not need to attach itself to an existing program. Worms almost always cause at least some harm to the network, even if only by consuming bandwidth, whereas viruses almost always corrupt or modify files on a targeted computer.

To see the full article -
https://en.wikipedia.org/wiki/Computer_worm

CryptoLocker virus - (source: *Wikipedia*) is a ransomware trojan which targeted computers running Microsoft Windows, believed to have first been posted to the Internet on 5 September 2013. CryptoLocker propagated via infected email attachments, and via an existing botnet; when activated, the malware encrypts certain types of files stored on local and mounted network drives using RSA public-key cryptography, with the private key stored only on the malware's control servers. The malware then displays a message which offers to decrypt the data if a payment (through either Bitcoin or a pre-paid cash voucher) is made by a stated deadline, and threatened to delete the private key if the deadline passes. If the deadline is not met, the malware offered to decrypt data via an online service provided by the malware's operators, for a significantly higher price in Bitcoin.

Although CryptoLocker itself is readily removed, files remained encrypted in a way which researchers considered infeasible to break. Many said that the ransom should not be paid, but did not offer any way to recover files; others said that paying the ransom was the only way to recover files that had not been backed up. Some victims claimed that paying the ransom did not always lead to the files being decrypted.

CryptoLocker was isolated in late-May 2014 via *Operation Tovar*—which took down the *Gameover ZeuS* botnet that had been used to distribute the malware. During the operation, a security firm involved in the process obtained the database of private keys used by CryptoLocker, which was in turn used to build an online tool for recovering the keys and files without paying the ransom. It is believed that the operators of CryptoLocker successfully extorted a total of around $3 million from victims of the trojan. Other instances of encryption-based ransomware that have followed have used the "CryptoLocker" name (or variations), but are otherwise unrelated.

To see the full article -
https://en.wikipedia.org/wiki/CryptoLocker

Cyber-Attack - (source: *Wikipedia*) is any type of offensive maneuver employed by individuals or whole organizations that targets computer information systems, infrastructures, computer networks, and/or personal computer devices by various means of malicious acts, usually originating from an anonymous source that either steals, alters, or destroys a specified target by hacking into a susceptible system. These can be labelled as either a Cyber campaign, cyberwarfare or cyberterrorism in different context. Cyber-attacks can range from installing spyware on a PC to attempts to destroy the infrastructure of entire nations. Cyber-attacks have become increasingly sophisticated and dangerous as the *Stuxnet worm* recently demonstrated.

To see the full article - *https://en.wikipedia.org/wiki/Cyber-attack*

Denial-of-Service Attack (source: *Wikipedia*) In computing, a *denial-of-service* (DoS) attack is an attempt to make a machine or network resource unavailable to its intended users, such as to temporarily or indefinitely interrupt or suspend services of a host connected to the Internet. A *distributed denial-of-service* (DDoS) is where the attack source is more than one—and often thousands—of unique IP addresses.

Criminal perpetrators of DoS attacks often target sites or services hosted on high-profile web servers such as banks, credit card payment gateways; but motives of revenge, blackmail or activism can be behind other attacks.

To see the full article - *https://en.wikipedia.org/wiki/Denial-of-service_attack*

NOTE: A recent DDoS was perpetrated by Anonymous hacktivists to thwart the recruiting efforts of ISIS through their website and social media. (Read more at *http://www.mirror.co.uk/news/technology-science/technology/anonymous-hacktivists-attack-isis---5130966*)

Email Spoofing - (source: *Wikipedia*) is the creation of email messages with a forged sender address. It is easy to do because the core protocols do not have any mechanism for authentication. It can be accomplished from within a LAN or from an external environment using Trojan horses. Spam and phishing emails typically use such spoofing to mislead the recipient about the origin of the message.

To see the full article – *https://en.wikipedia.org/wiki/Email_spoofing*

Firewall - (source: *Wikipedia*) a network security system that monitors and controls the incoming and outgoing network traffic based on an applied security rules. A firewall typically establishes a barrier between a trusted, secure internal network and another outside network, such as the Internet, that is assumed to not be secure or trusted.

Firewalls are often categorized as either *network firewalls* or *host-based firewalls*:

- **Network firewalls** are a software appliance running on general purpose hardware or hardware-based firewall computer appliances that filter traffic between two or more networks.

- **Host-based firewalls** provide a layer of software on one host that controls network traffic in and out of that single machine. Routers that pass data between networks contain firewall components and can often perform basic routing functions as well, Firewall appliances may also offer other functionality to the internal network they protect such as acting as a DHCP or VPN server for that network.

To see the full article -
https://en.wikipedia.org/wiki/Firewall_(computing)

Keyboard Loggers - (source: *Wikipedia*) *Keystroke logging*, often referred to as *keylogging* or *keyboard capturing*, is the action of recording (or logging) the keys struck on a keyboard, typically in a covert manner so that the person using the keyboard is unaware that their actions are being monitored. It has uses in the study of human–computer interaction. There are numerous keylogging methods, ranging from hardware and software-based approaches to acoustic analysis.

To see the full article –
https://en.wikipedia.org/wiki/Keystroke_logging

Malware – (source: *Wikipedia*) Short for *malicious software*, is any software used to disrupt computer operation, gather sensitive information, or gain access to private computer systems. Malware is defined by its malicious intent, acting against the requirements of the computer user, and does not include software that causes unintentional harm due to some deficiency. The term *badware* is sometimes used, and applied to both true (malicious) malware and unintentionally harmful software.

Malware may be stealthy, intended to steal information or spy on computer users for an extended period without their knowledge, as for example *Regin*, or it may be designed to cause harm, often as sabotage (e.g., *Stuxnet*), or to extort payment (*CryptoLocker*). 'Malware' is an umbrella term used to refer to a variety of forms of hostile or intrusive software, including *computer viruses, worms, trojan horses, ransomware, spyware, adware, scareware*, and other malicious programs. It can take the form of *executable code, scripts, active content*, and other software. Malware is often disguised as, or embedded in, non-malicious files. As of 2011, the majority of active malware threats were worms or trojans rather than viruses.

In law, malware is sometimes known as a computer contaminant, as in the legal codes of several U.S. states.

Spyware or other malware is sometimes found embedded in programs supplied officially by companies, e.g., downloadable from websites, that appear useful or attractive, but may have, for example, additional hidden tracking functionality that gathers marketing statistics. An example of such software, which was described as illegitimate, is the *Sony rootkit*, a Trojan embedded into CDs sold by Sony, which silently installed and concealed itself on purchasers' computers with the intention of preventing illicit copying; it also reported on users' listening habits, and unintentionally created vulnerabilities that were exploited by unrelated malware.

Software such as *antivirus*, *antimalware*, and *firewalls* are used to protect against activity identified as malicious, and to recover from attacks.

To see the full article -
https://en.wikipedia.org/wiki/Malware

Paypal – (source: *Wikipedia*) *PayPal Holdings, Inc.* is an American company operating a worldwide online payments system. Online money transfers serve as electronic alternatives to traditional paper methods like checks and money orders. PayPal is one of the world's largest internet payment companies. The company operates as an acquirer, performing payment processing for online vendors, auction sites and other commercial users, for which it charges a fee. For more information, you may also visit their website: *https://www.paypal.com.*

Personally Identifiable Information (PII) – (source: GSA Website in the appendix of OMB M-10-23 (Guidance for Agency Use of Third-Party Website and Applications)) the definition of PII was updated to include the following:

'Personally Identifiable Information (PII). The term "PII," as defined in OMB Memorandum M-07-1616 refers to information that can be used to distinguish or trace an individual's identity, either alone or when combined with other personal or identifying information that is linked or linkable to a specific individual. The definition of PII is not anchored to any single category of information or technology. Rather, it requires a case-by-case assessment of the specific risk that an individual can be identified. In performing this assessment, it is important for an agency to recognize that non-PII can become PII whenever additional information is made publicly available — in any medium and from any source — that, when combined with other available information, could be used to identify an individual.'

*Simply put, if you can figure out who the data pertains to because there are one or more details that identify it, **it is PII**.*

To see the full article -
http://www.gsa.gov/portal/content/104256

Phishing -
(source: *Wikipedia*) is the attempt to acquire sensitive information such as usernames, passwords, and credit card details (and sometimes, indirectly, money),

often for malicious reasons, by masquerading as a trustworthy entity in an electronic communication. The word is a *neologism* created as a homophone of fishing due to the similarity of using fake bait in an attempt to catch a victim. Communications purporting to be from popular social web sites, auction sites, banks, online payment processors or IT administrators are commonly used to lure unsuspecting victims. Phishing emails may contain links to websites that are infected with *malware*. Phishing is typically carried out by *email spoofing* or instant messaging, and it often directs users to enter details at a fake website whose look and feel are almost identical to the legitimate one. Phishing is an example of *social engineering* techniques used to deceive users, and exploits the poor usability of current web security technologies. Attempts to deal with the growing number of reported phishing incidents include legislation, user training, public awareness, and technical security measures. Many websites have now created secondary tools for applications, like maps for games, but they should be clearly marked as to who wrote them, and users should not use the same passwords anywhere on the internet.

Phishing is a continual threat that keeps growing to this day. The risk grows even larger in social media such as Facebook, Twitter, Myspace etc. Hackers commonly use these sites to attack persons using these media sites in their workplace, homes, or public in order to take personal and security information that can affect the user and the company (if in a workplace environment). Phishing is used to portray trust in the user since the user may not be able to tell that the site being visited or program being used is not real, and when this occurs is when the hacker has the chance to access the personal information such as passwords, usernames, security codes, and credit card numbers among other things.

List of phishing types

Phishing - An attempt to acquire information such as usernames, passwords, and credit card details by masquerading as a trustworthy entity in an electronic communication. In October 2013, emails purporting to be from American Express were sent to an unknown number of recipients. A simple DNS change could have been made to thwart this spoofed email, but American Express failed to make any changes.

Spear phishing - Phishing attempts directed at specific individuals or companies have been termed spear phishing.[43] Attackers may gather personal information about their target to increase their probability of success. This technique is, by far, the most successful on the internet today, accounting for 91% of attacks.

Clone phishing - A type of phishing attack whereby a legitimate, and previously delivered, email containing an attachment or link has had its content and recipient address(es) taken and used to create an almost identical or cloned email. The attachment or link within the email is replaced with a malicious version and then sent from an email address spoofed to appear to come from the original sender. It may claim to be a resend of the original or an updated version to the original. This technique could be used to pivot (indirectly) from a previously infected machine and gain a foothold on another machine, by exploiting the social trust associated with the inferred connection due to both parties receiving the original email.

Whaling - Several recent phishing attacks have been directed specifically at senior executives and other high profile targets within businesses, and the term whaling has been coined for these kinds of attacks. In the case of whaling, the masquerading web page/email will take a more serious executive-level form. The content will be crafted to target an upper manager and the person's role in the company. The content of a whaling attack email is often written as a legal subpoena, customer complaint, or executive issue. Whaling scam emails are designed to masquerade as a critical business email, sent from a legitimate business authority. The content is meant to be tailored for upper management, and usually involves some kind of falsified company-wide concern. Whaling phishermen have also forged official-looking FBI subpoena emails, and claimed that the manager needs to click a link and install special software to view the subpoena.

To see the full article -
https://en.wikipedia.org/wiki/Phishing

Ransomware - (source: *Wikipedia*) a type of malware that restricts access to the computer system that it infects, and demands a ransom paid to the creator(s) of the malware in order for the restriction to be removed. Some forms of ransomware encrypt files on the system's hard drive (cryptoviral extortion, a threat originally envisioned by Adam Young and Moti Yung), while some may simply lock the system and display messages intended to coax the user into paying.

To see the full article -
https://en.wikipedia.org/wiki/ Ransomware

Rootkit – (source: Wikipedia) A rootkit is a stealthy type of software, typically malicious, designed to hide the existence of certain processes or programs from normal methods of detection and enable continued privileged access to a computer. The term rootkit is a concatenation of "root" (the traditional name of the privileged account on UNIX operating systems) and the word "kit" (which refers to the software components that implement the tool). The term "rootkit" has negative connotations through its association with *malware*.

Rootkit installation can be automated, or an attacker can install it once they've obtained root or Administrator access. Obtaining this access is a result of direct attack on a system (i.e.), exploiting a known vulnerability (such as privilege escalation) or a password (obtained by cracking or social engineering). Once installed, it becomes possible to hide the intrusion as well as to maintain privileged access. The key is the root or Administrator access. Full control over a system means that existing software can be modified, including software that might otherwise be used to detect or circumvent it.

Rootkit detection is difficult because a rootkit may be able to subvert the software that is intended to find it. Detection methods include using an alternative and trusted operating system, behavioral-based methods, signature scanning, difference scanning, and memory dump analysis. Removal can be complicated or practically impossible, especially in cases where the rootkit resides in the kernel; reinstallation of the operating system may be the only available solution to the problem. When dealing with firmware rootkits, removal may require hardware replacement, or specialized equipment.

To see the full article - *https://en.wikipedia.org/wiki/Rootkit*

Scareware - (source: *Wikipedia*) included into the class of malware known as Rogueware, comprises several classes of ransomware or scam software with malicious payloads, usually of limited or no benefit, that are sold to consumers via certain unethical marketing practices. The selling approach uses social engineering to cause shock, anxiety, or the perception of a threat, generally directed at an unsuspecting user. Some forms of spyware and adware also use scareware tactics.

A tactic frequently used by criminals involves convincing users that a virus has infected their computer, then suggesting that they download (and pay for) fake antivirus software to remove it. Usually the virus is entirely fictional and the software is non-functional or malware itself. According to the Anti-Phishing Working Group, the number of scareware packages in circulation rose from 2,850 to 9,287 in the second half of 2008. In the first half of 2009, the APWG identified a 585% increase in scareware programs.

To see the full article -
https://en.wikipedia.org/wiki/Scareware

Shadow Volume Copy - (source: *Wikipedia*) (also known as *Volume Snapshot Service, Volume Shadow Copy Service* or *VSS*) is a technology included in *Microsoft Windows* that allows taking manual or automatic backup copies or snapshots of computer files or volumes, even when they are in use. It is implemented as a Windows service called the Volume Shadow Copy service. A software VSS provider service is also included as part of Windows to be used by Windows applications. Shadow Copy technology requires the file system to be NTFS to be able to create and store shadow copies. Shadow Copies can be created on local and external (removable or network) volumes by any Windows component that uses this technology, such as when creating a scheduled *Windows Backup* or automatic *System Restore* point.

To see the full article -
https://en.wikipedia.org/wiki/Shadow_Copy

Shareware- (source: *Wikipedia*) is a type of proprietary software which is provided (initially) free of charge to users, who are allowed and encouraged to make and share copies of the program, which helps to distribute it. The word "shareware" is a *portmanteau* combining the words "share" and "software". Shareware is often offered as a download from an Internet website or as a compact disc included with a magazine.

There are many types of shareware, and while they may not require an initial up-front payment, all are intended to generate revenue in one way or another. Some limit use to personal non-commercial purposes only, with purchase of a license required for use in a business enterprise. The software itself may be limited in functionality or be time-limited. Or it may remind you that payment would be appreciated.

Shareware is available on all major personal computer platforms. Titles cover a very wide range of categories including: business, software development, education, home, multimedia, design, drivers, games, and utilities. Because of its minimal overhead and low cost, the shareware model is often the only one practical for distributing non-free software for abandoned or orphaned platforms such as the Atari ST and Amiga.

The term shareware is used in contrast to open-source software, in which the source code is available for anyone to inspect and alter, and freeware, which is software distributed at no cost to the user but without source code being made available. Note that two types of shareware, *donationware* and *freemiums*, are also types of freeware.

To see the full article -
https://en.wikipedia.org/wiki/Shareware

Social Engineering – (source: *Wikipedia*) Social engineering, in the context of information security, refers to psychological manipulation of people into performing actions or divulging confidential information. A type of confidence trick for the purpose of information gathering, fraud, or system access, it differs from a traditional "con" in that it is often one of many steps in a more complex fraud scheme.

The term "social engineering" as an act of psychological manipulation is also associated with the social sciences, but its usage has caught on among computer and information security professionals.[

To see the full article -
https://en.wikipedia.org/wiki/Social_engineering_(security)

Spam- (source: *Wikipedia*) **SPAM** commonly refers to:

- *Spam* (electronic), unsolicited or undesired electronic messages
  - *Email spam*, unsolicited, undesired, or illegal email messages
  - *spam messages*, unsolicited, undesired, or illegal messages in general (private messages on websites, SMS, messenger etc...)

To see the full article -
https://en.wikipedia.org/wiki/Spam

StuxNet – (source: *Wikipedia*) A *computer worm* that was discovered in June 2010 edited by NSA and the Israeli unit 8200. It was designed to attack industrial *programmable logic controllers* (PLCs).

PLCs allow the automation of electromechanical processes such as those used to control machinery on factory assembly lines, amusement rides, or centrifuges for separating nuclear material. Exploiting four *zero-day flaws*, Stuxnet functions by targeting machines using the Microsoft Windows operating system and networks, then seeking out Siemens Step7 software. Stuxnet reportedly compromised Iranian PLCs, collecting information on industrial systems and causing the fast-spinning centrifuges to tear themselves apart. Stuxnet's design and architecture are not domain-specific and it could be tailored as a platform for attacking modern SCADA and PLC systems (e.g., in automobile or power plants), the majority of which reside in Europe, Japan and the US. Stuxnet reportedly ruined almost one-fifth of Iran's nuclear centrifuges.

Stuxnet has three modules: a *worm* that executes all routines related to the main payload of the attack; a *link file* that automatically executes the propagated copies of the worm; and a *rootkit* component responsible for hiding all malicious files and processes, preventing detection of the presence of Stuxnet.

Stuxnet is typically introduced to the target environment via an infected *USB flash drive*. The worm then propagates across the network, scanning for Siemens Step7 software on computers controlling a PLC. In the absence of both criteria, Stuxnet becomes dormant inside the computer. If both the conditions are fulfilled, Stuxnet introduces the infected rootkit onto the PLC and Step7 software, modifying the codes and giving unexpected commands to the PLC while returning a loop of normal operations system values feedback to the users.

To see the full article - *https://en.wikipedia.org/wiki/Stuxnet*

SWOT Analysis (alternatively **SWOT matrix**) (source – *Wikipedia*) is a structured planning method used to evaluate the strengths, weaknesses, opportunities and threats involved in a project or in a business venture. A SWOT analysis can be carried out for a product, place, industry or person. It involves specifying the objective of the business venture or project and identifying the internal and external factors that are favorable and unfavorable to achieve that objective. Some authors credit SWOT to Albert Humphrey, who led a convention at the Stanford Research Institute (now SRI International) in the 1960s and 1970s using data from Fortune 500 companies. However, Humphrey himself does not claim the creation of SWOT, and the origins remain obscure. The degree to which the internal environment of the firm matches with the external environment is expressed by the concept of strategic fit.

- *Strengths*: characteristics of the business or project that give it an advantage over others.
- *Weaknesses*: characteristics that place the business or project at a disadvantage relative to others.
- *Opportunities*: elements that the project could exploit to its advantage.
- *Threats*: elements in the environment that could cause trouble for the business or project.

Identification of SWOTs is important because they can inform later steps in planning to achieve the objective.

First, the decision makers should consider whether the objective is attainable, given the SWOTs. If the objective is not attainable a different objective must be selected and the process repeated.

Users of SWOT analysis need to ask and answer questions that generate meaningful information for each category (strengths, weaknesses, opportunities, and threats) to make the analysis useful and find their competitive advantage.

To see the full article -
https://en.wikipedia.org/wiki/SWOT_analysis

System Restore - (source: *Wikipedia*) is a feature in *Microsoft Windows* that allows the user to revert their computer's state (including system files, installed applications, *Windows Registry*, and system settings) to that of a previous point in time, which can be used to recover from system malfunctions or other problems. First included in Windows ME, it has since been included in all following desktop versions of Windows released since, excluding the Windows Server.

In prior Windows versions it was based on a file filter that watched changes for a certain set of file extensions, and then copied files before they were overwritten. An updated version of System Restore introduced by Windows Vista uses the *Shadow Copy* service as a backend (allowing block-level changes in files located in any directory on the volume to be monitored and backed up regardless of their location) and allows System Restore to be used from the *Windows Recovery Environment* in case the Windows installation no longer boots at all.

To see the full article -
https://en.wikipedia.org/wiki/System_Restore

Trojans - (source: *Wikipedia*) A Trojan horse, or Trojan, in computing is generally a non-self-replicating type of malware program containing malicious code that, when executed, carries out actions determined by the nature of the Trojan, typically causing loss or theft of data, and possible system harm. The term is derived from the Ancient Greek story of the large wooden horse used to trick defenders of Troy into taking warriors concealed in the horse into their city in ancient Anatolia. The use of this name references how computer Trojans often employ a form of social engineering, presenting themselves as routine, useful, or interesting in order to persuade victims to install them on their computers.

A Trojan often acts as a backdoor, contacting a controller which can then have unauthorized access to the affected computer. While Trojans and backdoors are not easily detectable by themselves, computers may appear to run slower due to heavy processor or network usage. Malicious programs are classified as Trojans if they do not attempt to inject themselves into other files (computer virus) or otherwise propagate themselves (worm). A computer may host a Trojan via a malicious program that a user is duped into executing (often an e-mail attachment disguised to be unsuspicious, *e.g.*, a routine form to be filled in), or by drive-by download.

To see the full article -
https://en.wikipedia.org/wiki/Trojan_horse_(computing)

USB Flash Drive – (source: *Wikipedia*) A USB flash drive, also known under a variety of other names, is a data storage device that includes flash memory with an integrated Universal Serial Bus (USB) interface. USB flash drives are typically removable and rewritable, and physically much smaller than an optical disc. Most weigh less than 30 grams (1.1 oz). As of January 2013, drives of up to 512 gigabytes (GB) were available. A one-terabyte (TB) drive was unveiled at the 2013 Consumer Electronics Show and became available later that year. Storage capacities as large as 2 TB are planned, with steady improvements in size and price per capacity expected. Some allow up to 100,000 write/erase cycles, depending on the exact type of memory chip used, and have a 10-year shelf storage time.

USB flash drives are often used for the same purposes for which floppy disks or CDs were used, i.e., for storage, data back-up and transfer of computer files. They are smaller, faster, have thousands of times more capacity, and are more durable and reliable because they have no moving parts. Additionally, they are immune to electromagnetic interference (unlike floppy disks), and are unharmed by surface scratches (unlike CDs). Until about 2005, most desktop and laptop computers were supplied with floppy disk drives in addition to USB ports, but floppy disk drives have been abandoned due to their lower capacity compared to USB flash drives.

USB flash drives use the USB mass storage standard, supported natively by modern operating systems such as Windows, Linux, OS X and other Unix-like systems, as well as many BIOS boot ROMs. USB drives with USB 2.0

support can store more data and transfer faster than much larger optical disc drives like CD-RW or DVD-RW drives and can be read by many other systems such as the Xbox 360, PlayStation 3, DVD players and in a number of handheld devices such as smartphones and tablet computers, though the electronically similar SD card is better suited for those devices.

A flash drive consists of a small printed circuit board carrying the circuit elements and a USB connector, insulated electrically and protected inside a plastic, metal, or rubberized case which can be carried in a pocket or on a key chain, for example. The USB connector may be protected by a removable cap or by retracting into the body of the drive, although it is not likely to be damaged if unprotected. Most flash drives use a standard type-A USB connection allowing connection with a port on a personal computer, but drives for other interfaces also exist. USB flash drives draw power from the computer via the USB connection. Some devices combine the functionality of a digital audio player with USB flash storage; they require a battery only when used to play music.

Flash drives come in various shapes and sizes, sometimes bulky or novelty, such as the shape of *ikura gunkan-maki.*

To see the full article -

https://en.wikipedia.org/wiki/USB_flash_drive

n.b.: Newer computers and flash drives support USB v3.0 which supports faster read/write speeds than USB v2.0.

Windows Registry - (source: *Wikipedia*) is a hierarchical database that stores configuration settings and options on Microsoft Windows operating systems. It contains settings for low-level operating system components and for applications running on the platform that have opted to use the Registry. The kernel, device drivers, services, SAM, user interface and third-party applications can all make use of the Registry. The Registry also provides a means to access counters for profiling system performance.

When first introduced with Windows 3.1, Windows Registry's primary purpose was to store configuration information for COM-based components. With the introduction of Windows 95 and Windows NT, its use was extended to tidy up the profusion of per-program INI files that had previously been used to store configuration settings for Windows programs. It is not a requirement for a Windows application to use Windows Registry—for example, .NET Framework applications use XML files for configuration, while portable applications usually keep their configuration data within files in the folder where the application executable resides.

To see the full article -
https://en.wikipedia.org/wiki/Windows_Registry

Acceptable Use Policy Template

1.0 Overview

<Company Name>'s intentions for publishing an Acceptable Use Policy are not to impose restrictions that are contrary to <Company Name>'s established culture of openness, trust and integrity. <Company Name> is committed to protecting <Company Name>'s employees, partners and the company from illegal or damaging actions by individuals, either knowingly or unknowingly.

Internet/Intranet/Extranet-related systems, including but not limited to computer equipment, software, operating systems, storage media, network accounts providing electronic mail, WWW browsing, and FTP, are the property of <Company Name>. These systems are to be used for business purposes in serving the interests of the company, and of our clients and customers in the course of normal operations. Please review Human Resources policies for further details.

Effective security is a team effort involving the participation and support of every <Company Name> employee and affiliate who deals with information and/or information systems. It is the responsibility of every computer user to know these guidelines, and to conduct their activities accordingly.

2.0 Purpose

The purpose of this policy is to outline the acceptable use of computer equipment at <Company Name>. These rules are in place to protect the employee and <Company

Name>. Inappropriate use exposes <Company Name> to risks including virus attacks, compromise of network systems and services, and legal issues.

3.0 Scope

This policy applies to employees, contractors, consultants, temporaries, and other workers at <Company Name>, including all personnel affiliated with third parties. This policy applies to all equipment that is owned or leased by <Company Name>.

4.0   Policy

4.1   General Use and Ownership

1. While <Company Name>'s network administration desires to provide a reasonable level of privacy, users should be aware that the data they create on the corporate systems remains the property of <Company Name>. Because of the need to protect <Company Name>'s network, management cannot guarantee the confidentiality of information stored on any network device belonging to <Company Name>.

2. Employees are responsible for exercising good judgment regarding the reasonableness of personal use. Individual departments are responsible for creating guidelines concerning personal use of Internet/Intranet/Extranet systems. In the absence of such policies, employees should be guided by departmental policies on personal use, and if there is any uncertainty, employees should consult their supervisor or manager.

3. <Company Name> recommends that any information that users consider sensitive or vulnerable be encrypted. For guidelines on information classification, see <Company Name>'s Information Sensitivity Policy. For guidelines on encrypting email and documents, go to <Company Name>'s Awareness Initiative.

4. For security and network maintenance purposes, authorized individuals within <Company Name> may monitor equipment, systems and network traffic at any time, per <Company Name>'s Audit Policy.

5. <Company Name> reserves the right to audit networks and systems on a periodic basis to ensure compliance with this policy.

4.2 Security and Proprietary Information

1. The user interface for information contained on Internet/Intranet/Extranet-related systems should be classified as either confidential or not confidential, as defined by corporate confidentiality guidelines, details of which can be found in Human Resources policies. Examples of confidential information include but are not limited to: company private, corporate strategies, competitor sensitive, trade secrets, specifications, customer lists, and research data. Employees should take all necessary steps to prevent unauthorized access to this information.

2. Keep passwords secure and do not share accounts. Authorized users are responsible for the security of their passwords and accounts. System level passwords should be changed quarterly, user level passwords should be changed every six months.

3. All PCs, laptops and workstations should be secured with a password-protected Screensaver with the automatic activation feature set at 10 minutes or less, or by logging-off (control-alt-delete for Win2K users) when the host will be unattended.

4. Use encryption of information in compliance with <Company Name>'s Acceptable Encryption Use policy.

5. Because information contained on portable computers is especially vulnerable, special care should be exercised. Protect laptops in accordance with the "Laptop Security Tips".

6. Postings by employees from a <Company Name> email address to newsgroups should contain a disclaimer stating that the opinions expressed are strictly their own and not necessarily those of <Company Name>, unless posting is in the course of business duties.

7. All hosts used by the employee that are connected to the <Company Name> Internet/Intranet/Extranet, whether owned by the employee or <Company Name>, shall be continually executing approved virus-scanning software with a current virus database unless overridden by departmental or group policy.

8. Employees must use extreme caution when opening e-mail attachments received from unknown senders, which may contain viruses, e-mail bombs, or Trojan horse code.

4.3. Unacceptable Use

The following activities are, in general, prohibited. Employees may be exempted from these restrictions during the course of their legitimate job responsibilities (e.g., systems administration staff may have a need to disable the network access of a host if that host is disrupting production services).

Under no circumstances is an employee of <Company Name> authorized to engage in any activity that is illegal under local, state, federal or international law while utilizing <Company Name>-owned resources.

The lists below are by no means exhaustive, but attempt to provide a framework for activities which fall into the category of unacceptable use.

System and Network Activities

The following activities are strictly prohibited, with no exceptions:

1. Violations of the rights of any person or company protected by copyright, trade secret, patent or other intellectual property, or similar laws or regulations, including, but not limited to, the installation or distribution of "pirated" or other software products that are not appropriately licensed for use by <Company Name>.

2. Unauthorized copying of copyrighted material including, but not limited to, digitization and distribution of photographs from magazines, books or other copyrighted sources, copyrighted music, and the installation of any copyrighted software for which <Company Name> or the end user does not have an active license is strictly prohibited.

3. Exporting software, technical information, encryption software or technology, in violation of international or regional export control laws, is illegal. The appropriate

management should be consulted prior to export of any material that is in question.

4. Introduction of malicious programs into the network or server (e.g., viruses, worms, Trojan horses, e-mail bombs, etc.).

5. Revealing your account password to others or allowing use of your account by others. This includes family and other household members when work is being done at home.

6. Using a <Company Name> computing asset to actively engage in procuring or transmitting material that is in violation of sexual harassment or hostile workplace laws in the user's local jurisdiction, including any type of pornographic material.

7. Making fraudulent offers of products, items, or services originating from any <Company Name> account.

8. Making statements about warranty, expressly or implied, unless it is a part of normal job duties.

9. Effecting security breaches or disruptions of network communication. Security breaches include, but are not limited to, accessing data of which the employee is not an intended recipient or logging into a server or account that the employee is not expressly authorized to access, unless these duties are within the scope of regular duties. For purposes of this section, "disruption" includes, but is not limited to, network sniffing, pinged floods, packet spoofing, denial of service, and forged routing information for malicious purposes.

10. Port scanning or security scanning is expressly prohibited unless prior notification to <Company Name> is made.

11. Executing any form of network monitoring which will intercept data not intended for the employee's host, unless this activity is a part of the employee's normal job/duty.

12. Circumventing user authentication or security of any host, network or account.

13. Interfering with or denying service to any user other than the employee's host (for example, denial of service attack).

14. Using any program/script/command, or sending messages of any kind, with the intent to interfere with, or disable, a user's terminal session, via any means, locally or via the Internet/Intranet/Extranet.

15. Providing information about, or lists of, <Company Name> employees to parties outside <Company Name>.

Email and Communications Activities

1. Sending unsolicited email messages, including the sending of "junk mail" or other advertising material to individuals who did not specifically request such material (email spam).

2. Any form of harassment via email, telephone or paging, whether through language, frequency, or size of messages.

3. Unauthorized use, or forging, of email header information.

4. Solicitation of email for any other email address, other than that of the poster's account, with the intent to harass or to collect replies.

5. Creating or forwarding "chain letters", "Ponzi" or other "pyramid" schemes of any type.

6. Use of unsolicited email originating from within <Company Name>'s networks of other Internet/Intranet/Extranet service providers on behalf of, or to advertise, any service hosted by <Company Name> or connected via <Company Name>'s network.

7. Posting the same or similar non-business-related messages to large numbers of Usenet newsgroups (newsgroup spam).

4.4. Blogging

1. Blogging by employees, whether using <Company Name>'s property and systems or personal computer systems, is also subject to the terms and restrictions set forth in this Policy. Limited and occasional use of <Company Name>'s systems to engage in blogging is acceptable, provided that it is done in a professional and responsible manner, does not otherwise violate <Company Name>'s policy, is not detrimental to <Company Name>'s best interests, and does not interfere with an employee's regular work duties. Blogging from <Company Name>'s systems is also subject to monitoring.

2. <Company Name>'s Confidential Information policy also applies to blogging. As such, Employees are prohibited from revealing any <Company Name>

confidential or proprietary information, trade secrets or any other material covered by <Company Name>'s Confidential Information policy when engaged in blogging.

3. Employees shall not engage in any blogging that may harm or tarnish the image, reputation and/or goodwill of <Company Name> and/or any of its employees. Employees are also prohibited from making any discriminatory, disparaging, defamatory or harassing comments when blogging or otherwise engaging in any conduct prohibited by <Company Name>'s Non-Discrimination and Anti-Harassment policy.

4. Employees may also not attribute personal statements, opinions or beliefs to <Company Name> when engaged in blogging. If an employee is expressing his or her beliefs and/or opinions in blogs, the employee may not, expressly or implicitly, represent themselves as an employee or representative of <Company Name>. Employees assume any and all risk associated with blogging.

5. Apart from following all laws pertaining to the handling and disclosure of copyrighted or export controlled materials, <Company Name>'s trademarks, logos and any other <Company Name> intellectual property may also not be used in connection with any blogging activity

5.0 Enforcement

Any employee found to have violated this policy may be subject to disciplinary action, up to and including termination of employment and legal action.

6.0 Definitions

Term Definition

Blogging   Writing a blog. A blog (short for *weblog*) is a personal online journal that is frequently updated and intended for general public consumption.

Spam   Unauthorized and/or unsolicited electronic mass mailings.

7.0 Revision History

> **NOTE: PRIOR to using AUP, please have it reviewed by legal counsel.**

---

*"Give me six hours to chop down a tree and
I will spend the first four sharpening the axe."*
— Abraham Lincoln

Worthwhile websites to visit
for more info on
Cybercrime and Online Safety Tips

<u>Note</u>: In order to maintain legibility of the referenced websites, in some cases, we have broken them over multiple lines to make them easier to read. If you copy only the first line of the URL, you will not always get to the cited web address. Please makes sure to enter the complete listing on all lines shown in *italics.*

<u>Organizations:</u>

FBI Cyber Crime
> *https://www.fbi.gov/about-us/investigate/cyber*

Federal Emergency Management Agency ....*www.fema.gov*

Federal Trade Commission .... *http://www.ftc.gov*

Institute for Business and Home Safety (IBHS)
> *https://www.disastersafety.org/disastersafety*
> */open-for-business-ez*

Krebs on Security .... *http://krebsonsecurity.com*

National Security Agency......................*https://www.nsa.gov*

NJ Cybersecurity.............................*http://www.cyber.nj.gov*

Small Business Administration (NJ) ....*www.sba.gov/nj*

Small Business Development Centers of NJ
> *http://www.njsbdc.com*

StaySafeOnline (National Cyber Security Alliance)
https://www.staysafeonline.org/stay-safe-online
/protect-your-personal-information
/id-theft-and-fraud

US Computer Emergency Readiness Team
https://www.us-cert.gov

US Dept. Homeland Security – Combating Cyber Crime
http://www.dhs.gov/topic/combating-cyber-crime

US Dept. of Justice (reporting)
http://www.justice.gov/criminal-ccips
/reporting-computer-internet-related-or-intellectual-
property-crime

US Dept. of Labor – PII.... *http://www.dol.gov/dol/ppii.htm*

Commercial Sites:

Belarc Advisor ....*http://www.belarc.com*

Cybercrime Survival Guide: Website Security Solutions
http://www.symantec.com/tv/products
/details.jsp?vid=3395695511001

Datto Backup ....*http://www.datto.com*

Equifax (Credit Bureau)...........................*www.equifax.com*

Experian (Credit Bureau).......................*www.experian.com*

HIPAA Secure Now
http://www.hipaasecurenow.com

Holzsager Technology Services, LLC
http://www.tech4now.com

Norton: Top Prevention Tips
http://us.norton.com/prevention-tips/article

PII Protect *http://www.tech4now.com/pii-protect*

Sophos – Naked Security
https://nakedsecurity.sophos.com

StorageCraft .... *www.storagecraft.com*

Symantec TV ....*http://www.symantec.com/tv*

TransUnion (Credit Bureau)...............*www.transunion.com*

Related Articles:

Banking Securely Online
https://www.us-cert.gov/sites
/default/files/publications
/Banking_Securely_Online07102006.pdf

Cyber Threats to Mobile Phones
https://www.us-cert.gov/sites
/default/files/publications
/cyber_threats_to_mobile_phones.pdf

Disposing of Devices Safely
https://www.us-cert.gov/sites
/default/files/publications
/DisposeDevicesSafely_0.pdf

Hackers Steal Data on 10.5 Million Excellus Healthcare
Customers (InfoSecurity Magazine Online)
http://www.infosecurity-magazine.com/news
/hackers-steal-data-105-million/

How a Remote Town in Romania has become Cybercrime
Central (WIRED Magazine Online)
http://www.wired.com/2011/01/ff_hackerville_romania

Password Security, Protection, and Management
https://www.us-cert.gov/sites
/default/files/publications
/PasswordMgmt2012.pdf

Malvertising: More Than a Nuisance
http://www.cyber.nj.gov/nj-cyberlog/2015/9/23
/malvertising-more-than-a-nuisance

Prepare to Get Hit Warns FBI Cybercrime Boss (InfoSecurity
Magazine Online)
http://www.infosecurity-magazine.com/news
/fbi-highlights-cybercrime

Ten Ways to Improve the Security of a New Computer
https://www.us-cert.gov/sites
/default/files/publications
/TenWaystoImproveNewComputerSecurity.pdf

The Risks of Using Portable Devices
https://www.us-cert.gov/sites
/default/files/publications
/RisksOfPortableDevices.pdf

Quick QUIZ ANSWER

Quick QUIZ: Below is a recent scam mail we received in our office. How many concerns can you identify in this message?

Subject: Urgent Trip

Apologize for disturbing your moments, i came down here to Istanbul (TURKEY) for a mission program last night unfortunately on my way going back to the hotel room i got mugged all phones, cash, passport and and valuable items are in the bag they went it. The Embassy has really been helping issues for giving me a temporary passport.

Before I can head out for my flight I have to settle the hotel the bill am owing right now, i contact my bank and they get back to me with a sad reply! it will take up to 3-5 working days to access funds in my account. My flight will soon take off. I need your help/financial loan of € 2,550 Euro to sort out our hotel bill, will pay back once back home safe.

Will be very grateful, any help is appreciated

Kind Regards

Michael

The issues pointed out are not an exhaustive list of all issues, but will identify most of them:

- No Salutation in the letter (e.g., "Dear Fred").

- No use of pronoun in first sentence – "I apologize…"

- "disturbing your moments" is not normal English, it seems more like a Google Translate clause. Most would say, "Sorry to bother you, but…"

- Note the first person pronoun, "I," is in lower case a few times.

- Throughout the body of the letter, punctuation is sporadic at best. Most of the paragraph is a run-on sentence.

- The word "and" is repeated.

- In general, the wording throughout the body of the letter is not similar to spoken English.

- In second paragraph, "am owing," flags this as a non-native speaker. The person who purportedly wrote this is from NJ. (Even though many in the US would question our use of English, it IS still better than the example shown.)

- If this message were sent in Morse code, I could rationalize the omission of so many words that would have us think this was in English, but, alas, it isn't.

- The only way possible to communicate with this person is by responding to the email. If you were borrowing somebody's computer to send an URGENT message, would email be your first choice? Keep in mind, if you call this person at the phone number you have in your contact list, you will actually speak with him. If you do, obviously, the scam is blown.

- If you were to ask someone to wire money, wouldn't you give them an address or place to remit it? We only know that this person went to Istanbul, Turkey; however, who knows where Michael is now?

Although there are many "Red Flags," we feel this should give you a valid example of how to recognize a scam spam email message.

References

Rubin, Steven. S. and A. Jonathan Trafimow (2015, August 15). Outside Counsel, Expert Analysis: Counsel's Capacity To Control Cybersecurity Costs. *New York Law Journal, Vol. 254(29).*

NOTES:

NOTES:

NOTES:

An Invitation to the Reader

Many of my clients and colleagues have asked if I have a decent *Acceptable Use Policy* to share with them, as well as a simple outline that I could share which explains how to setup a Disaster Recovery Plan or Business Continuity Plan. So, I took it as a personal task to create that resource.

Now, you hold in your hand, a common sense, easy to read guide to get you thinking and on the road to protecting your business in the best ways possible. I am not saying that you cannot hire a consultant to help you prepare everything from soup to nuts, but if you have the ambition and the interest, you can transform your business from the common to the exceptional by implementing some basic concepts on a consistent basis presented in this book.

Will your business survive a disaster? There's no telling whether you will take our suggestions to heart or skip some of the more challenging parts, but we can say with confidence that reading this book will get you started on the road to preparedness. It is our wish that it will take you further than that, but it's really up to you.

If you found this book useful or valuable, we would love to hear your feedback. If we receive enough stories from you, we can improve this book and release a second edition giving more details on what to look out for, what works and what doesn't. If you have additional tips or insights that we haven't considered, please feel free to share them.

Again, the more aware you are of how you can anticipate change, the more successful you will be in business. I hope you have benefitted from this book. I'd love to hear from you with your thoughts, successes, and horror stories as well. Thank you.

Contact me at:

Holzsager Technology Services, LLC
Fred W. Holzsager
fred@tech4now.com
(201) 797-5050
13-15 Broadway
Fair Lawn, NJ 07410

www.tech4now.com

PII Protect

If you are interested in learning more about protecting your business from vulnerabilities created by the presence of **Personally Identifiable Information (PII)**, either give us a call at **(201) 797-5050** or visit our website's dedicated page to Protecting PII

www.tech4now.com/pii-protect

to request more information or enroll in **PII Protect**.

On that page, you will find useful information describing what PII is, what it costs businesses, how *PII Protect* can help you in the event of a breach as well as help reduce your "attack surface" by documenting security methods you can implement to reduce the accessible PII present on your business' systems.

As a thank you for buying this book, we will extend a 10% (ten percent) discount on the *PII Protect Program* offered through **Holzsager Technology Services, LLC**. Simply indicate you bought the book and would like the discount, give the code "PII10".

This is our thank you for taking the steps on your own to reduce the likelihood of experiencing a breach and causing yourself and others hardship through identity theft.

To learn more, view our brief video:

https://youtu.be/KW4ygpq8Udg

Book Order Form

If you enjoyed this book, share it with others! Use this form to order extra copies for friends, colleagues, clients, or members of your association. Please allow 2-4 weeks for delivery.

Quantity Discounts:

1-9 copies = $14.95, 10-49 copies = $13.95 each

50-99 copies = $12.95 each

100 or more copies = Call for discounts and wholesale prices

Information:

Name: _____

Company: _____

Address: _____

City: _____

State/Province: _____

ZIP/Postal Code: _____

# of copies _____ @ $_____ Total: $_____

Add shipping and handling @ $3 per book: $_____

Tax must be applied to all sales (NJ Sales Tax 7%) $_____
(If your Association is Tax Exempt, please include a copy of your Tax Exemption certificate from the State.)

Please make check or money order payable to:

Holzsager Technology Services, LLC
13-15 Broadway
Fair Lawn, NJ 07410
(201) 797 - 5050